A Civil War Scrapbook

I Was There Too!

HISTORY *Colorado*

FULCRUM
GOLDEN, COLORADO

Library of Congress Cataloging-in-Publication Data

A Civil War scrapbook : I was there too! / History Colorado.
    p. cm.
 Includes bibliographical references and index.
 ISBN 978-1-55591-668-8 (pbk.)
 1. United States--History--Civil War, 1861-1865--Juvenile literature. I. History Colorado.
E468.C64 2012
973.7--dc23

                    2011042043

Printed in Canada
0 9 8 7 6 5 4 3 2 1

Fulcrum Publishing
4690 Table Mountain Dr., Ste. 100
Golden, CO 80403
800-992-2908 • 303-277-1623
www.fulcrumbooks.com

This book supports the following national standards:
National Social Studies Standards Civics: NSS-C.5-8.3, Principles of Democracy
Economics: NSS-EC.5-8.1, Scarcity
Geography: NSS-G.k-12.4, Human Systems
History: NSS-USH.5-12.4, Era 4 Expansion and Reform, 1801–1861
NSS-USH.5-12.5, Era 5 Civil War and Reconstruction, 1850–1877
National Standards for Language Arts: NL-ENG.k-12.2, Understanding the Human Experience
NL-ENG.k-12.8, Developing Research Skills
National Standards for Art Education: NA-T.5-8.5, Researching by Using Cultural and Historical Information to Support Improvised and Scripted Scenes

Adapted from the curriculum guide *My Civil War Scrapbook*
Project director: Bobbe Hultin
Colorado State Historian: William J. Convery
Writer: Marilyn Lindenbaum
Editors: Steve Grinstead and David Wetzel
Designer: Julie Rudofsky, In House Design

CONTENTS

The Civil War 4

Slavery and the Civil War 8

The Beginning 9

Soldier's Story 10

Manassas (Bull Run) (July 21, 1861) 12

   The Second Battle of Manassas 14

Missouri's Role in the War 17

Wilson's Creek (August 10, 1861) 18

Technology and the War 20

Medicine and the War 22

Glorieta Pass (March 26–28, 1862) 24

Women in the Civil War 28

Harpers Ferry (September 12–15, 1862) 30

Music and the Civil War 32

Antietam (September 17, 1862) 36

Emancipation Proclamation 39

Civil War Gazette 40

Gettysburg (July 1–3, 1863) 42

The Power of Words 45

Animals Go to War Too 46

Honey Springs (July 17, 1863) 48

The Changing Flags 50

Lexington, Virginia 52

New Market (May 15, 1864) 54

The Final Year 56

The End of War 57

The Beginning of Change (Reconstruction) 58

Time Line 59

Glossary of Civil War Terms 60

Bibliography 62

Credits 63

Index 64

THE CIVIL WAR

The American Civil War took place from 1861 to 1865. When it was over, more than 620,000 Americans had died. Thousands of mules and horses died of overwork, starvation, battle wounds, or disease. Entire cities were destroyed. Families lost their homes, farms, belongings, and loved ones.

A **civil war** is a war between the citizens of the same country. You may wonder what would make fellow countrymen—and countrywomen—fight against each other. Even close friends and family members chose sides and faced each other in battle.

WHY?

The Civil War was a long time in the making. People first came to settle in the American colonies for independence, freedom, and the promise of a good life lived off the rich, open lands. Especially in the South, the warmer climate and fertile soil led to the growth of major crops like sugar, rice, tobacco, and cotton. As the demand for these goods grew, so did the need for larger farms or plantations and cheap labor to work in the fields. This economic problem led to the practice of **slavery**.

Slavery was a source of debate from the beginning. Many felt the practice was cruel and immoral. Slaves were considered property to be bought and sold and were often beaten, poorly fed, and denied an education. Slave owners argued that without slave labor, the demand for goods could not be met. Because some of them owned slaves, the men who wrote the Constitution left it up to the individual states to decide about slavery.

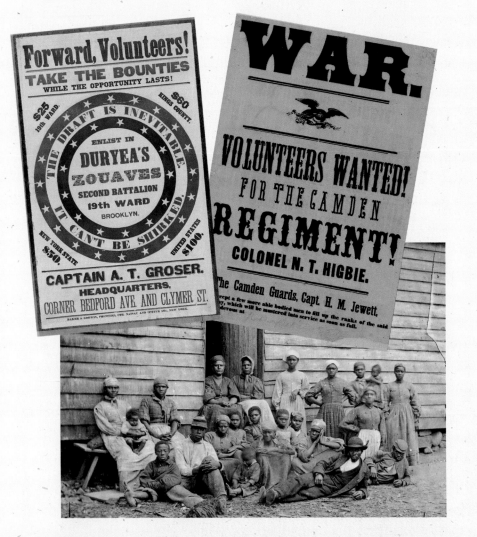

In the years leading up to the Civil War, the debate over slavery became very heated. Those who wanted to end or abolish it were called **abolitionists**. They wrote newspaper articles and books, made speeches, and signed petitions to persuade others to join their cause. Those who depended on slave labor for their businesses argued that ending slavery would ruin the economy of the South. They warned that northerners would suffer through severe shortages of jobs and goods, and impossibly high prices.

Events Leading Up to the Civil War

* In 1820, Congress tried to keep slavery from spreading to the western territories by drawing an imaginary line across the country all the way to the Pacific Ocean. The so-called Missouri Compromise line allowed the creation of slave states to the south and free states to the north.

* The discovery of gold in California in 1849 created a huge gold rush. The debate over statehood for California and Oregon led to new arguments over whether slavery should exist in the West.

* Congress passed the Fugitive Slave Law in 1850. It gave slave owners the power to recover runaway slaves from free states and even allowed them to claim free black people who had never been slaves as their property.

* In 1854, Congress created two new territories, Nebraska and Kansas. The arguments between supporters of slavery and those against it were fierce. They even turned violent in Kansas and its neighboring state, Missouri.

* In 1857, the US Supreme Court ruled that slave owners could take their slave property anywhere in the United States—even into states where slavery was illegal. In the words of Supreme Court chief justice Roger B. Taney, black people had "no rights that whites were bound to respect."

* In November 1860, Abraham Lincoln was elected president of the United States. On December 20, 1860, South Carolina became the first of eleven southern states to withdraw from the United States and form their own country, the Confederate States of America.

DRED SCOTT

Slave

One of the most important turning points leading up to the Civil War was the court case of a Missouri slave who sued for his freedom. His name was Dred Scott. The case went all the way to the Supreme Court. The Court ruled that, as a slave, Scott had no legal rights and was regarded by the law as the owner's property. This outraged the people who wanted to abolish slavery.

HARRIET BEECHER STOWE

Author

Outraged at the injustices of the 1850 Fugitive Slave Law, Harriet Beecher Stowe wrote a novel called *Uncle Tom's Cabin*. Published in 1851, it became the best-selling book of its time and very plainly presented the cruelties of slavery. It fueled the fiery debate even more. Abraham Lincoln met Stowe in 1862 and greeted her with these words: "So you're the little woman who wrote the book that made this Great War!"

FREDERICK DOUGLASS

Escaped slave

In 1818, Frederick Douglass was born into slavery in Maryland. By 1838, he had taught himself to read and write, and he escaped to freedom. His *Narrative of the Life of Frederick Douglass, an American Slave* was an inspiration to those fighting against slavery. His true-life description of the evils of slavery was a powerful argument against the continuing practice of human ownership.

ABRAHAM LINCOLN

16th President of the United States

Born in Kentucky in 1809, Abraham Lincoln was self-educated, grew up farming, and later became a lawyer in Illinois. In 1858, Lincoln and Stephen Douglas both ran for US Senate from that state. Although Lincoln lost the election, his antislavery speeches and statements from the debates were published in a book and helped him win the nomination for president in 1860. His election was the one event, more than any other, that pushed the nation toward civil war.

JEFFERSON DAVIS

President of the Confederate States of America

Jefferson Davis was born in Kentucky, graduated from West Point, and served as US secretary of state and as a senator from Mississippi. In 1861, when Mississippi seceded from the United States, Davis quit the Senate and was elected to a six-year term as president of the Confederacy. After the Civil War, he was charged with treason but never went to trial.

ROBERT E. LEE

Confederate general

Born and raised in Virginia, Robert E. Lee had strong ties to the state that became the capital of the Confederacy. He was a graduate of West Point and a career soldier. Abraham Lincoln asked him to lead the Union army, but Lee declined, going home to Virginia when it left the Union in 1861. He became the leader of the Confederate army. Lee was an able commander, but the shortage of people and resources in the South led to his surrender on April 9, 1865.

ULYSSES S. GRANT

Union general

Ulysses S. Grant was born in Ohio in 1822. He graduated from West Point but returned to his father's leather tannery to work. When war broke out in 1861, he was appointed by the governor of Ohio to command its volunteer regiment. In March 1864, Lincoln asked Grant to become the general-in-chief for the Union, replacing George McClellan. His tireless **campaign** against Lee, combined with his partnership with General William T. Sherman, brought victory to the Union.

CLARA BARTON

Nurse

Born in Massachusetts in 1821, Clara Barton was educated at home and at the age of 15 began to teach school. When the Civil War broke out, she was working in Washington, DC. Clara heard about the shortage of medical supplies on the battlefield. She started an organization to collect much-needed bandages and was given a pass to travel with the army ambulances into battle. In the midst of fighting, she bandaged wounds and comforted the dying.

SLAVERY AND THE CIVIL WAR

Susie King Taylor

Susie King Taylor was born into slavery in Georgia in 1848. She was sent to Savannah, where she secretly learned to read and write. A free black woman, Mrs. Woodhouse, had a school in her home. Susie and her brother hid their books in plain paper and joined twenty-five or thirty others in Mrs. Woodhouse's kitchen school. Susie went on to start her own school for black children and adults, to serve black troops as an unpaid nurse and cook, and, later, to bring recognition to African American heroes of the Civil War.

Henry "Box" Brown

Henry Brown was born into slavery in Virginia. While working in Richmond in a tobacco factory, he planned his escape. With the help of others, he had himself shipped to Philadelphia in a box! His friends in Richmond made arrangements for a white abolitionist to receive the package. Despite the twenty-seven-hour journey, the box bouncing around and even sitting upside down for part of the time, Henry made it. He became famous giving speeches for the American Anti-Slavery Society and retelling his own story. After that, he was forever known as Henry "Box" Brown.

Harriet Tubman

Harriet Tubman was born into slavery in Maryland and worked as a field hand. In 1849, afraid she was about to be sold, she escaped on foot, following the North Star toward Pennsylvania and freedom. Once in Philadelphia, she worked and saved her money. The next year, she returned to lead her sister and others to the North. Harriet Tubman returned nineteen times to help more than 300 people escape from slavery. She liked to say that, as a conductor on the Underground Railroad, she "never lost a passenger." Tubman also went on to help the Union army during the war, working as a nurse, cook, and spy.

Underground Railroad

Despite its name, the Underground Railroad was not a real train system but a secret organization of people who helped slaves escape to free states and even other countries. The conductors were people who led them along parts of the journey, and the stations were safe places to rest, be fed, and get help. Some had secret rooms, tunnels, and hidden boats nearby. Some slaves traveled under the false bottom of a wagon, some traveled by foot, using the stars for guidance, and some rowed a boat across a still river under the cover of darkness. Whichever way a slave chose to escape, the decision was a dangerous and courageous one.

The Beginning

As the presidential election of 1860 approached, there were 33 states in the Union: 11 slave states, 17 free states, and 5 border states between them.

Southern states felt that being forced to give up slavery interfered with their right to govern themselves according to the will of their citizens—in other words, "states' rights." They also argued that slavery was recognized in the Constitution and was thus granted to individual states. Finally, they believed that states had the right to withdraw from the United States and form their own country, just as the Founding Fathers had created a new country in defiance of England.

Northerners didn't agree. They believed that the United States was formed with the idea of majority rule. It was not within states' rights, they argued, to leave the Union simply because a state or its citizens didn't like the ruling government. The United States couldn't survive as a nation if states came and went with every disagreement.

Shortly after Abraham Lincoln's election, eleven southern states **seceded** from the United States and formed a new country, the Confederate States of America. They inaugurated Jefferson Davis as president and wrote a new constitution. Both North and South seemed to know that war was inevitable and that neighbors, friends, and even families would divide as they took sides and supported what they thought was right.

The Confederacy took over a number of forts and military posts in the South. Fort Sumter, in Charleston Harbor, was still controlled by the US military, and its commander, Major Robert Anderson, refused to give up his post. On April 12, 1861, Confederate troops fired on the fort and forced its **surrender**.

The Civil War had begun.

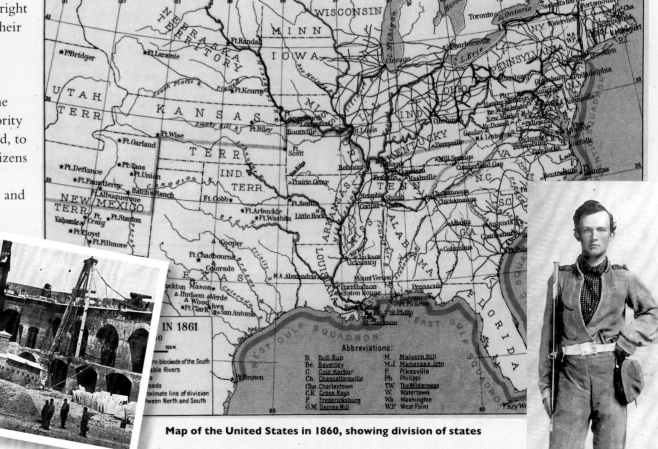

Fort Sumter

Map of the United States in 1860, showing division of states

Abbreviations:
B. Bull Run
Be. Beverley
C. Cold Harbor
Ch. Chancellorsville
Cha. Charlestown
C.K. Cross Keys
F. Fredericksburg
G.M. Gaines Mill
M. Malvern Hill
M.J. Manassas Jctn.
P. Pikesville
Ph. Philippi
T.W. TheWilderness
W. Watertown
Wa. Washington
W.P. West Point

SOLDIER'S STORY

Citizen Soldiers

Many army leaders in the Civil War trained together at military schools and had fought alongside each other in earlier wars. But the regular soldiers who made up most of the armies on both sides were citizen soldiers. They had little military training, and most had never fought in a war. Some believed in the cause and volunteered. Some saw war as an adventure or just needed the money. Early in the war, many men wore their own clothes into battle, and **regiments** designed their own battle flags. The lack of uniforms and changing flags caused confusion and disastrous mistakes on the battlefield.

Conscription

As the war went on, it became harder and harder to get people to volunteer. Both sides resorted to **conscription**, or a draft—requiring young men to serve in the army. Rich people could be excused or pay someone else to serve in their place. This caused a lot of bitterness among the poor, who had no choice but to serve. Angry workers and immigrants in New York City staged a bloody riot against the draft in July 1864.

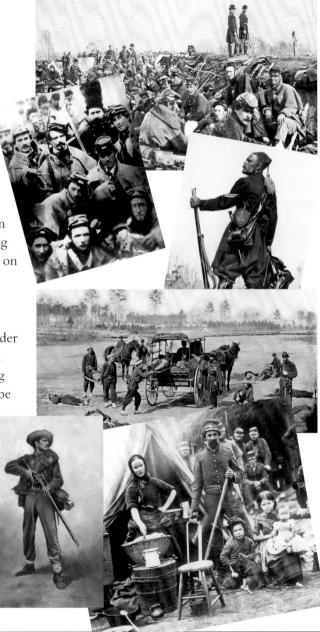

Deserters

Because citizen soldiers were not used to the discipline of the military, armies on both sides had problems with behavior and even desertion. Some men went home to plant or harvest crops. Shortages of decent food and clean water, combined with the horrors of war, sent others home in fear or frustration. Punishments ranged from the humorous to the deadly: Some were forced to wear a large, heavy barrel, hung from straps like suspenders. Others were shot.

Zouaves

Can you imagine wearing baggy red pants into battle? The **Zouaves** were known for their fierce fighting and bravery, but they wore colorful uniforms and turbans. Eventually, they toned down their outfits somewhat, realizing that the bright colors made them much more visible targets.

Child Soldiers

No identification papers were needed to sign up for the army. Although the required age was 18, boys could easily lie about their age and often had friends or family who would go along with their stories. Teenagers rushed to join up because they thought it was going to be a great adventure. None, it seems, understood the violent and terrible nature of what they were signing up for.

Drummer Boys

Many young boys were allowed to sign up as musicians. Flutes played lively tunes as an accompaniment to marching, but trumpets and drums signaled movement in drills and battles. Drummer boys, especially, sounded out orders during the confusion on smoky battlefields. The sight of the drummer boy let troops know where their companies were, so drummer boys were often targets of enemy fire.

Johnny Clem, the most famous drummer boy of the Civil War, ran away from home and tried to join the army at the age of 9. He tagged along with a Michigan company until he was enlisted as an 11-year-old drummer boy. At the battle of Shiloh, an **artillery** shell destroyed his drum, and he was nearly wounded by gunfire, and he became known as Johnny Shiloh. Because drummer boys were so young, they were among the last survivors of the Civil War. Johnny Clem stayed in the army until his retirement in 1916. He died in 1937 at the age of 85.

Prisoners of War

Both armies maintained prisoner-of-war camps. Those taken in battle were crowded into small, guarded areas. Poor shelter, filthy living conditions, and a lack of clean water caused many prisoners to die of disease, dehydration, and starvation. The most terrible prisoner-of-war camp was Andersonville, Georgia. In the end, 13,000 of the 45,000 men imprisoned there died from exposure to the brutal summer heat or disease. Andersonville's commander was the only person tried and executed for war crimes after the Civil War.

The Friendship of Enemies

Soldiers from both sides often found themselves very close to the enemy, just across a field or a creek. Sometimes they met on the battlefield, tending to their dead and wounded after a battle. This was especially true in winter, when the enemy might be camped close by. An odd kind of friendship emerged from these meetings. Soldiers shared stories, traded items like tobacco, coffee, or blankets, sang songs, and joked about their circumstances. They came to see the enemy as very much like themselves, young people caught up in an unstoppable moment in history. Although these meetings did not keep them from plunging into battle against each other, they did occasionally lead to desertion or an agreement not to shoot at each other in the next battle unless their regiments were commanded to **charge**.

I was there too!

Finding both Union and Confederate soldiers in their home in Gettysburg, the McCreary family invited them all to dinner. "Now that they had stopped fighting, both sides seemed to be on the best of terms, and laughed and chatted like old comrades."

—Albertus McCreary, age 15

Manassas (Bull Run)

July 21, 1861

Why Here?

After the attack on Fort Sumter, both the North and South got ready to do battle. A quiet town in Virginia suddenly became very important. Manassas Junction was less than 30 miles southwest of Washington, DC, and only 90 miles north of Richmond, the new capital of the Confederacy.

* Both sides wanted to control the two train lines that met there, since they could use the trains to move soldiers and supplies.
* Many northerners believed a quick victory in Manassas would lead to the capture of Richmond.
* By July 1861, 20,000 Confederate soldiers were camped at Manassas to guard the railroad junction. Another 11,000 camped nearby, at the arsenal in Harpers Ferry.
* 35,000 Union soldiers went to Washington and prepared to march into Virginia; many had only **volunteered** for 90 days and would be free to go home by the end of July.

Lincoln met with Union General Irvin McDowell, who advised waiting until the men were better trained. But Lincoln was anxious to march "on to Richmond" and told McDowell, "You are **green**, it's true, but they are green, also; you are all green alike."

In the Neighborhood

In 1861, farms and plantations filled the rolling hills and woods around Manassas. Bull Run creek ran through the peaceful farmland. For families living there, the railroad junction had brought a better way to get their harvest to bigger markets. Now, knowing the battle was coming, many residents left to take cover with friends or family who lived away from Manassas. Excited over what they thought would be a short clash and an easy win, some Washington citizens, congressmen, and reporters rode out by carriage to picnic and watch the Union victory. They had no idea what was coming.

The Big Picture

McDowell and his troops attacked at dawn on July 21. His battle plan seemed to work at first, although both armies were disorganized, confused by the different uniforms and flags and unable to see through the thick smoke on the battlefield. The Union managed to push the Confederates back to Henry House Hill, but more southerners arrived, led by Thomas J. "Stonewall" Jackson. Supposedly, Confederate General Bee pointed Jackson out to his troops, saying, "Look at Jackson standing there like a…stone wall!" giving Jackson his famous nickname. When more Confederates arrived from Harpers Ferry, the exhausted Union soldiers retreated. Southern forces were too tired to chase after them, and the battle was over.

HERO VILLAIN

In 1861, Rose O'Neal Greenhow was a popular hostess in Washington, DC, and a Confederate spy. She used her charm to learn important secrets and pass them on through young women who delivered coded messages concealed in their hair or clothing. Rose was eventually convicted as a spy and sent back to Richmond, where she was greeted as a hero. Jefferson Davis sent her to England to get information and help for the Confederacy. On her way back, her ship ran aground off the coast of North Carolina. Trying to reach shore by rowboat, Rose O'Neal Greenhow drowned, weighed down by $2,000 in gold she was carrying.

The battles at Manassas are also known as the battles of Bull Run. The Confederates named battles for the nearest town, while the Union named battles after nearby rivers or streams.

What went wrong

The Confederates knew when the Union army was going to march into Virginia toward Manassas. They had received the information from Rose O'Neal Greenhow, their spy in Washington. By the time the Union soldiers were ready for battle, Confederate General Beauregard had prepared for their arrival and sent for the troops in Harpers Ferry. Those troops marched to the rail line and rode the train right into Manassas, arriving just in time to join the battle and discourage the worn-out Union troops. Trying to retreat, Union soldiers found their way blocked by picnickers, who had been shocked by the bloody fighting and were trying to get back to the safety of Washington. The confusion caused panic among the soldiers, and many of them dropped their guns and ran down the road, trying to get away.

Dead on Bull Run battlefield

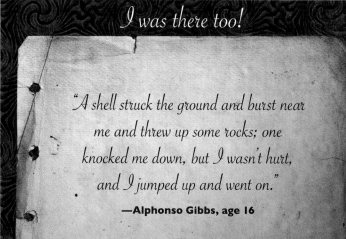

I was there too!

"A shell struck the ground and burst near me and threw up some rocks; one knocked me down, but I wasn't hurt, and I jumped up and went on."

—Alphonso Gibbs, age 16

The Rest of the Story

Both the North and South under-estimated their enemy, each thinking that the other side didn't have the spirit or skill to fight. Both sides expected a few shots to be fired and the other army to give up and go home. No one saw the long, bloody war that was coming.

Rose O'Neal Greenhow's spy who brought information to Manassas was 16-year-old Bettie Duvall. Bettie hid the message in her hair. "She…let fall the longest and most beautiful roll of hair that I have ever seen on a human head." Out came a small black silk purse, containing the coded message: "McDowell has certainly been ordered to advance on the sixteenth. R.O.G."

Wilmer McLean and his family lived on a plantation near Manassas. General Beauregard made his headquarters there. After the battle, the family moved to Appomattox Court House, a small town where the Civil War would eventually come to an end, again at the home of Wilmer McLean.

Judith Henry was too old and ill to leave her home on Henry House Hill. She became the first civilian killed at the first battle of Manassas, when her home was destroyed in the fighting.

Stonewall Jackson got his nickname during the first battle of Manassas. He also encouraged his men to give a terrifying yell when they attacked. Soldiers used this **rebel yell** for the rest of the war.

New York Congressman Alfred Ely was among the citizens who rode out to Manassas to witness the battle. The Confederates captured him, sent him to prison in Richmond, and released him on Christmas Day, 1861, in a prisoner exchange. He later wrote a book about his experiences as a prisoner of war.

The Second battle of Manassas

August 28–30, 1862

Soldiers fought another battle at Manassas Junction a year later. Lincoln had appointed General John Pope to lead the fight in Virginia. Pope and his soldiers had moved into Manassas Junction after the Confederates left to defend Richmond. They used the train lines to gather supplies for the battles to come. Confederate General Lee was determined to get rid of them. He divided his soldiers into two groups: one under Stonewall Jackson's command and the other under James Longstreet. Jackson and his men attacked first, making Pope think he could outnumber the enemy by sending all of his soldiers into battle. Just when the Union thought they had won, Longstreet's troops appeared over the hillside, firing cannons and attacking with new energy. Pope's exhausted men fell apart under the heavy fire, and the battle was lost. Pope's short career as commander of the Union army in Virginia was over.

Lesson Learned

Never underestimate your opponent's skill, especially when spirit and determination are involved.

CIVIL WAR ACTIVITY

Spy Tactics

Information is one of the most important keys to success in war. Without telephones or computers, military leaders in the Civil War depended on the telegraph, hot air balloons, written notes, and spoken messages. Spies were critical to finding out the enemy's plans and making battle strategies. **Sutlers**, tradesmen, shopkeepers, and even citizens who overheard plans could take the information to the army they supported. Women could move easily between camps because men were not accustomed to searching or questioning them. Posing as well-dressed wives or daughters looking for their loved ones, they could pass messages to soldiers from any camp. Spying required a person to be sly, crafty, and quick while staying calm and quiet. It could be very dangerous work.

The spies of the US Secret Service got their start during the Civil War. The Confederacy had its Signal Bureau sending coded messages from city to city. Suddenly both governments realized the importance of protecting their own information while trying to find out the enemy's. Newspapers often printed military movements and battle preparations. Robert E. Lee read every northern newspaper his spies could bring him. These reports helped him change troop movements and make new war strategies. He even planted a false story in the papers to mislead Union leaders about his own military maneuvers.

Project 1: Hidden Treasures

Ten objects are hidden in the clothing of these three Civil War ladies. Find them:

book   medicine   candle

scroll   sock   purse

scarf   coins

note   gloves

Project 2: Pass a Secret Message!

Here's what you'll need:
• A small piece of paper and a pencil

Step 1: Write these words on your paper: WE MEET AT DAWN! Put your initials at the bottom of the paper.

Step 2: Fold the paper and hide it in your clothing or shoes without being seen by anyone.

Step 3: Sometime during the day, slip your note to a designated adult. Don't let anyone see you!

CIVIL WAR ACTIVITY

Every Soldier Needs a Housewife!

Soldiers often had to repair holes or torn clothing while on the march. Most carried a simple sewing kit known as a "housewife." The folded packet contained cloth patches, buttons, pins, and needles and thread. It could be easily carried in a pocket and weighed very little.

Marching long distances through sometimes rough terrain and the violence of battle meant that tears and worn spots happened often and needed mending. "Housewives" were usually prepared by the wife, mother, or daughter of a soldier going off to war.

Project: Civil War Housewife

Here's what you'll need to make your own:
- 10" x 4" strip of felt
- 3 rectangles of different color felt, 3" x 4"
- Needle and thread
- 13" piece of cotton ribbon
- Buttons, needle and thread, 3 fabric patches

Step 1: Center the long strip of felt on top of the ribbon, and attach in the center with just a few stitches.

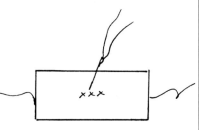

Step 2: Evenly space the small felt rectangles on top of the long strip of felt, and sew in place with a simple running stitch. Be sure to sew only three sides of each piece to form three pockets.

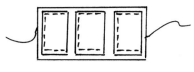

Step 3: Place the patches inside the top pocket, the buttons in the second pocket, and the needle and thread inside the third pocket.

Step 4: Fold in thirds and tie with the ribbon.
Some other things you can carry inside your housewife: Band-Aids, tissues, notes, and other small treasures.

Dear _____,

I wanted you to have this little "housewife" so that you

I will be thinking of you, and hope that

I look forward to the time when you come home.
Please write, and let me know _____

Love,

Just for Fun

Imagine your thoughts and feelings if you had made this housewife for a loved one going off to war. Fill in the blanks in this little note that you might have tucked inside when you presented it to your soldier.

MISSOURI'S ROLE IN THE WAR

Kansas, Missouri, and Slavery

All of Missouri was caught up in the argument over slavery. Missouri entered the Union as a slave state in 1820. To balance the power of slavery and antislavery states in Congress, Maine was admitted as a free state at the same time. Congress drew an imaginary dividing line between slave and free soil across the West from the western tip of Missouri's southern border. The so-called Missouri Compromise helped prevent civil war for about forty years. In the years leading up to the Civil War, bitter conflicts took place throughout the state over slavery between Missourians and antislavery settlers in neighboring Kansas. Some of these conflicts were violent. Both slave owners and antislavery groups, called **free soilers**, were murdered and their property destroyed. Some 200 people died in the violence known as "Bleeding Kansas" in the 1850s.

The Dred Scott Case

Slaves Dred Scott and his wife, Harriet, belonged to a Missouri woman, Irene Emerson. They had lived in Illinois and other free territories for a few years while working for Irene's husband, John, who was an army surgeon. One of their daughters was born in free **territory** before they returned to the slave state of Missouri. After John Emerson died, Dred Scott sued for his freedom. He argued that his long stay in a free territory was grounds for being set free. More than ten years of trials, verdicts, and retrials followed, leading all the way to the US Supreme Court. In 1857, the Court issued its verdict. Dred Scott was not entitled to his freedom. As a black slave, the court argued, he was considered property and not allowed to enjoy the rights and privileges of a US citizen. The mostly southern justices also ruled that prior laws passed to protect the territories from slavery were unconstitutional.

Even though Dred Scott was freed less than three months after the ruling, this judgment set off a firestorm of reactions all over the country. Abolitionists held public meetings to protest the "outrageous decision," while southern newspaper editorials praised it. President James Buchanan was happy to hide behind the Court's ruling, saying that the question of slavery would "be speedily and finally settled" by their decision. There was nothing final about it.

WILSON'S CREEK

August 10, 1861

WHY HERE?

You may wonder why Missouri was so important to both the Union and the Confederacy.

* St. Louis, "The Gateway to the West," was a valuable shipping center and entry point for western resources.
* The Mississippi and Missouri Rivers were needed for shipping and supplies.
* The area had a good population, rich farmlands, and other natural resources.
* It was the center of bitter conflicts over slavery.

Since it was a border state, many of Missouri's citizens wanted to stay neutral in the conflict. The governor and others, however, sided with the Confederacy. When President Lincoln asked Governor Claiborne Fox Jackson to call for Union volunteers, Jackson refused. He also ordered the Missouri State Guard to move against the US Arsenal in St. Louis. This led to a series of **skirmishes** and maneuvers that brought forces from both sides to Wilson's Creek on the morning of August 10, 1861.

In the Neighborhood

Wilson's Creek ran through farmlands. The Ray family had a house on a hillside across the valley from Oak Hill. John Ray was the postmaster. His house sat on the **wire road** that carried the telegraph and wagons across the countryside. The Ray household included a slave, Rhoda, and her four children. During the battle, they all hid in the basement, except for John Ray, who watched the fighting from his front porch. When it was over, the home was used as a Confederate hospital, with all the family and slaves helping to treat the wounded men.

THE BIG PICTURE

Union General Nathaniel Lyon was moving his army south from the state capital of Springfield in pursuit of Confederate forces, including the Missouri State Guard. The Confederates, led by Major General Sterling Price, were moving north, hoping to defeat Union troops and retake Missouri for the South. Each side planned a surprise attack, but rain forced the Confederates to camp near Wilson's Creek on the night of August 9. General Lyon planned to surround the Confederates by sending troops with Colonel Franz Sigel to attack from the enemy's rear while he brought his men up from the front. At first, all went according to plan. The Union troops moved ahead to the crest of Oak Hill, where fierce fighting took place.

I was there too!

Early in the morning, three of the Ray children were gathering their animals in the pasture when a Confederate soldier came by. "There's going to be fighting like hell in less than ten minutes!" They ran back to the house to warn the family, grabbed a pan of just-baked biscuits, and all scrambled to the basement where they stayed for six hours, until the battle was over.

—**From the stories of Olivia Ray Bruton**

HERO / VILLAIN

President Lincoln asked Missouri's Governor Jackson to recruit four regiments of soldiers when the Civil War began. Jackson refused. Instead, he ordered the Missouri State Guard to overtake the US Arsenal near St. Louis. To some Missourians, he was a hero, trying to protect the slave owners' rights. But to many others, his refusal to comply with Union policy caused years of bitter fighting and destruction.

The Rest of the Story

Wilson's Creek was the first major battle west of the Mississippi River. At the beginning of the war, in 1861, standard uniforms had not been issued to everyone, and every regiment had its own battle flag. Communication was poor, and many officers had little or no military training. What could have been a Union victory was ruined by mistaken identity and bad communication.

Colonel Sigel's retreat and the death of General Lyon led to the defeat of Union forces at Wilson's Creek. Even though the Confederacy won the battle, their forces and supplies were so diminished that they lost control of Missouri, and they never regained it.

Nathaniel Lyon was the first Union general killed in battle in the Civil War. His body was mistakenly left at the battlefield. Eventually, it was taken to the Ray family's house, wrapped in a bedspread belonging to Mrs. Ray, and returned by Confederate guards to Union headquarters.

The Rays were not physically injured by the battle, but all were left with lasting memories of the sights and sounds of war. Hungry soldiers took all of their supplies and animals and left their corn crop ruined in the battlefield.

What went wrong

Colonel Sigel mistakenly thought that nearby Confederate troops were Lyon's Union men. By the time he realized his mistake, his soldiers were under attack. He and his forces had to retreat, leaving General Lyon to fight—and eventually die—on what would later be known as "Bloody Hill."

Lesson Learned

Communication is key. Finding ways to give and get information is very important, whatever the situation.

TECHNOLOGY AND THE WAR

Railroads, steamboats, ironclad warships, repeating rifles and **minié balls**, Gatling guns, submarines, canned food, hot air balloons, and the telegraph: practical science was a big part of the Civil War.

Samuel Morse developed a communication method for the telegraph to transmit words by pressing dots and dashes into a piece of paper. The telegraph operator could put the patterns together to translate the message into words.

Abraham Lincoln was determined to understand and use every bit of technology he could to win the war.

* Hot air balloons were used to spy on enemy troops.
* Repeating rifles and better ammunition ended the war more quickly.
* Trains and steamboats moved troops and supplies where they were needed.
* Canned food improved the miserable diet of the soldier.

* When Lincoln took office, the War Department sent its messages by standing in line at the central telegraph office with everyone else! Later, Lincoln had a telegraph line put into the War Department near the White House so he could monitor each day's events and send orders.

The Morse Code Alphabet

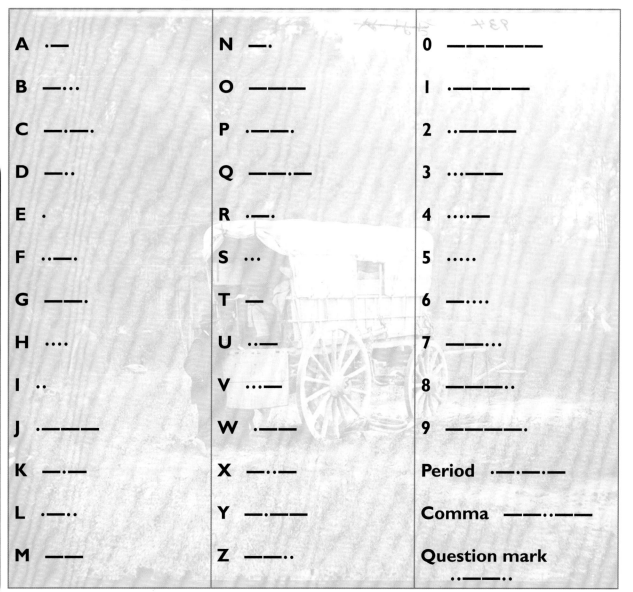

CIVIL WAR ACTIVITY

Project: Try It Yourself

Use the Morse code alphabet key to translate the following quote, and write it on the blank lines below. It is the first telegraphed message ever sent by Morse code!

.— .... . —   .... . — ....

—. — . — —..

.— — —. — .—. . ...—.

— — — —

— — —

— — — — — — —

Just for Fun

Try writing out the names of Abraham Lincoln's sons in dots and dashes:

Robert Todd Lincoln   Edward Lincoln
Willie Lincoln   Tad Lincoln

A	.—	**N**	—.	**0**	—————
B	—...	**O**	———	**1**	.————
C	—.—.	**P**	.——.	**2**	..———
D	—..	**Q**	——.—	**3**	...——
E	.	**R**	.—.	**4**	....—
F	..—.	**S**	...	**5**	.....
G	——.	**T**	—	**6**	—....
H	....	**U**	..—	**7**	——...
I	..	**V**	...—	**8**	———..
J	.———	**W**	.——	**9**	————.
K	—.—	**X**	—..—	**Period**	.—.—.—
L	.—..	**Y**	—.——	**Comma**	——..——
M	——	**Z**	——..	**Question mark**	..——..

MEDICINE AND THE WAR

When the Civil War began, no one believed it would last long. Each side thought the other one would quickly give up. Neither army was well prepared for the war's terrible casualties.

* More than 620,000 soldiers died.
* Two-thirds died of typhoid fever, malaria, dysentery, and tuberculosis.
* Unsanitary conditions caused diseases and infections.

Better Weapons

As technology improved, so did the weapons of war. Armies began using **rifle-muskets**. These had fine grooves inside the barrel that made them more accurate. This, along with the bullet known as the minié ball, led to terrible injuries. The ball's shape improved the speed and accuracy of the shot and tore through organs and bones on impact.

Dealing with Injuries

Amputation of limbs was the most common operation. The same instruments were used on every patient. Surgeries took place on tables or any flat surface, and chloroform was the usual anesthetic. Homes became military hospitals, and hospital flags flew over these houses and medical tents to avoid enemy attack.

By the end of the war, medical procedures on both sides had much improved:

* Armies appointed field medical directors, who supervised rapid pickup and transport of the wounded.
* The military enrolled women nurses to assist with care.
* Many civilian groups provided services and supplies to military hospitals.
* The US Sanitary Commission began hospital inspections. It also held auctions and events to raise money for supplies. (Lincoln donated his original draft of the Emancipation Proclamation to be auctioned.)

CIVIL WAR ACTIVITY

Downtime in the Army

Most battles of the Civil War happened in the spring, summer, and fall. Winter was a time for settling into winter quarters and waiting out the weather. Soldiers busied themselves with more lighthearted activities like music, making up stories, and playing games. Many carried cards or dice, and they gambled their pay in games of chance. If paper and pencil were available, simple game boards could be drawn, and buttons, pebbles, or sticks were used as playing pieces.

Connect the Dots

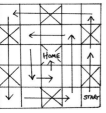

Players take turns drawing lines vertically or horizontally between two dots. If a player completes a box, that person puts their initials inside it. The game is over when all dots are connected. The player with the most boxes wins.

Board Game

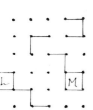

Each player starts with 4 pieces (stones, buttons, etc.). At least one die is required.

Players take turns throwing the dice and moving the correct number of spaces on the board, until the piece reaches the Home space. The first player to move all 4 pieces home wins the game. If a player lands on a square occupied by another player, the first player's piece must return to Start and begin again. Spaces marked with an **X** can be shared by the players.

Marbles

Using a stick, draw a circle on the ground, at least 3 feet in diameter.

- All players should have one large shooter marble, and 5 smaller marbles.
- Players place all small marbles somewhere in the circle.
- Players take turns shooting the large marble at the small ones, trying to roll them out of the circle.
- Players collect any marbles they are able to hit out of the circle.
- If a player hits a marble out, their turn continues.
- When all marbles are out of the circle, the player with the most marbles wins.

Project: Design Your Own Game

Here's what you'll need to create something fun:

- Pebbles, buttons, marbles, or small objects for playing pieces
- Dice or something you can use in place of dice **OR**
- Paper and pencil

Step 1: Decide what kind of game you would like to design. It can be a word game, a maze, a paper and pencil game, or a game you play with pieces.

Step 2: Write down the rules of the game. Players need to know how to play and win.

Step 3: If it is a board game, design the playing board, including Start and Finish.

Step 4: Try out the game with a friend to see if you need to make some changes.

GLORIETA PASS

March 26–28, 1862

WHY HERE?

The United States wanted to develop the land and resources of the West, and so did the Confederacy.

The West offered:

* Lots of open farmland for slavery to expand
* Rich mines of gold and other minerals in Colorado and California
* The important trade route of the Santa Fe Trail
* Hundreds of miles of Pacific Ocean coastline for shipping goods

New Mexico was still a territory. The Confederates hoped to make it another slave state.

In the Neighborhood

Glorieta Pass is a path through the Sangre de Cristo Mountains, narrowing at its western end in Apache Canyon. The Santa Fe Trail, the main route from the high plains to Santa Fe, ran through the pass, providing a useful trade route to New Mexico. Two stagecoach stops, Kozlowski's Ranch and Pigeon's Ranch, became important places for the armies to retreat, regroup, and wait for reinforcements. Because it was near the top of Glorieta Pass, some of the fiercest fighting took place at Pigeon's Ranch. Confederate supply wagons stood at Johnson's Ranch, near Apache Canyon.

THE BIG PICTURE

The Confederates moved quickly to take over federal forts and military supplies in the West. In 1862, General Henry Sibley marched an army of Texans into New Mexico. He won the first major battle at Valverde, near Fort Craig, then went on to capture Albuquerque and Santa Fe. The territorial governor, Henry Connelly, had called for volunteers to fight against the coming **rebels**. About 80 percent of the 4,000 volunteers who came forward were Hispanic men from local communities. Colorado sent a regiment of volunteers too. They marched 400 miles in thirteen days to reinforce Fort Union. In March 1862, Union troops met up with Confederate troops on the Santa Fe Trail. They engaged each other near Pigeon's Ranch. The Confederacy seemed to have won this three-day battle, but at the last minute, the tide turned.

HERO | VILLAIN

Union Major John Chivington was hailed as a hero for his role in the battle at Glorieta. But he is best remembered as the man responsible for the Sand Creek Massacre. On November 29, 1864, he led an attack on a peaceful village of Cheyenne and Arapaho Indians who had set up camp under the protection of the US government. More than 130 Indians were killed, 105 of them women and children. This was the beginning of fierce Indian wars with federal troops all over the West.

What went wrong

Volunteer soldiers from Colorado, led by Major John Chivington and guided by Colonel Manuel Chaves of the New Mexico Volunteers, discovered and destroyed more than seventy Confederate supply wagons carrying food and ammunition. Despite the Confederates' victories, without fresh horses and supplies they were forced to retreat. The supply wagons at Glorieta were not well placed or guarded. The Confederacy paid the price for its mistake, losing New Mexico and a chance at western expansion.

The Rest of the Story

Most Civil War battle maps do not include New Mexico, but the battle at Glorieta was later called the Gettysburg of the West. It turned the tide for Confederate defeat in the western territories.

Many Hispanic men in New Mexico were poor farmers and day workers. The army pay of $13 a month was very appealing, especially for defending lands that they hoped would someday become a state.

At least 10,000 Mexican Americans served in the Civil War. Some were treated with jealousy, disrespect, and discrimination. Often unable to speak English, they were given poor, outdated equipment. Yet they helped secure the territory with their courage, knowledge of the land, experience in battle, and willingness to help their new country.

Santos Benavides, the highest-ranking Mexican American officer in the Confederacy, achieved the rank of colonel.

Sergeant Alfred Peticolas was part of the Texas group. He became separated from them and found himself in the middle of the enemy Union camp. Taking a US coat from a dead soldier, he walked among the Union troops back to his Confederate line. He was never discovered.

I was there too!

"I had my horse killed in the battle of Valverde and I am now on foot. . .[T]he severity of the climate. . .the hardships of a march of a thousand miles over mountains. . .all the horrors that are witnessed on the battle field. . .I never had any conception of the hardships to be witnessed on such a trip until I had some experience in the matter."

—Ebineezer (Abe) Hanna, age 17, 4th Texas Regiment. Abe was the regimental historian and the youngest soldier killed at Glorieta.

Lesson Learned

Whoever controls the resources has the upper hand.

CIVIL WAR ACTIVITY

Letters from Home

The only connection a soldier had to home and family was through the mail. Letter writing was one of the few things that helped to pass the long days, weeks, and sometimes months between battles. Packages were especially welcomed, with special foods and new clothing. The Union army provided post office services to men in camp, including free postage for mail marked *Soldier's Letter* on the envelope. Sutlers sold letter paper, which was often printed with flags, eagles, and other patriotic symbols. As the war went on, paper was sometimes in short supply, especially for the Confederates, who suffered from shortages of all kinds. Letters sometimes were written on notebook paper, wallpaper, or wrappers that could serve as stationery.

Project: Writing Between the Lines

When paper was unavailable, soldiers used letters they had received and wrote in the empty spaces between the lines. Imagine you are a soldier and have received a letter from home. Try your hand at answering back by writing in between the lines.

Here's what you'll need:
• Written letter
• Pencil

Step 1: Take a look at the letter on the next page and read the message. You will notice the big spaces between the sentences. That is where you will write your letter back.

Step 2: Think about your answers to the questions in the letter and anything else a Civil War soldier might write back to the family. Soldiers often described their experiences in battle and tried to assure their families that they were safe and well.

Step 3: Using a pencil, write a return letter carefully between the lines of the original one. Try to use proper spelling and grammar in composing your message.

To My Dearest,

So much time has passed since I last heard from you. I hope that you are safe and that you have not been taken

ill by measles or dysentery. We hear so much about the sicknesses that are so dangerous to our boys at war. Life

here is quiet, but difficult. We are making clothes out of scraps of material that come from sacks of flour and

cornmeal. I hope the army is giving you enough food. We were lucky to buy sweet potatoes and chicken last week,

but mostly we have whatever vegetables and fruits we stored in September. Are you keeping warm? I sent a package

to you some time ago. Did you receive it? There was a small cake, some wool socks, and several pieces of soap. My

friend Margaret's son wrote that he was in a battle near Wilson's Creek, in Missouri. I think he is in your

regiment. Were you there? It sounded terrible. I am so worried that you will be wounded or worse. Please write back

as soon as you can to put my mind at ease. Stay safe and warm. Until we meet again,

Your sweetheart

WOMEN IN THE CIVIL WAR

A woman's life in 1860 was very different than a woman's life today. Women were not allowed to vote, and they were not encouraged to get an education. Married women could not own property unless it was through inheritance, had very few legal rights, and could not appear in court. Women in slavery were forbidden to learn to read or write, and they worked either as field hands or as house servants. They barely had time to raise their own children and often had their families sold away from them.

Still, many women participated in the war in meaningful and interesting ways. Women ran the farms and shops while the men served in uniform. Some cared for the sick and injured or advanced their side's causes as soldiers and spies.

Nurses

Many women served as nurses in the Civil War. Often working as volunteers, they assisted field doctors with their grim task of caring for the wounded and comforting the dying. Women helped with surgery and amputations, changed bandages, and tried to keep patients clean and fed. Even though most worked far behind the battle lines, the work was dangerous and constant under very difficult circumstances.

Dorothea Dix was in charge of the Union army nurses. She insisted that the women dress plainly in dark clothing without any jewelry. She also insisted that the nurses provide care for Union and Confederate soldiers alike. One of her nurses wrote about the injured Confederates: "Though enemies, they were nevertheless helpless, suffering human beings."

Spies

Belle Boyd and Rose O'Neal Greenhow were among the women who served as Confederate spies. Hiding battle plans in their hair, pinning notes to the inside of their aprons, and hanging medicine, letters, and socks from the wire hoops under their skirts, these women were able to pass on goods and information without being suspected. Since women were not seen as a danger, they could listen in on conversations in hotel lobbies or stores, and they could pass on important information they heard. If caught, most were not imprisoned but simply sent home.

Daughters of the Regiment and Vivandières

Women, who were not permitted to enlist, often stayed with regiments, providing encouragement, cooking, sewing, or writing letters for those who did not know how. These female helpers often supplied comfort to the injured and assisted behind the lines in battle. Called **vivandières**, they also acted as sutlers, selling tobacco, coffee, food, and whiskey. Sometimes they were the wives or daughters of officers. They often wore a female version of a uniform: a military jacket, skirt, and pants with leggings underneath. Kady Brownell tried to enlist alongside her husband but was turned away. She stayed with him as a daughter of the regiment and fought in battles.

"Braiding my hair very close, I put on a man's wig, and a false mustache, and by tucking my pantaloons in my boots...I managed to transform myself into a very presentable man."

Women as Soldiers in Disguise

Some women wanted to join the fight as soldiers.
They had many reasons:
* A deep belief in the cause
* A need for paying work
* Revenge for the death of a loved one
* To be near a brother or husband
* Excitement
* More freedom as a man

It was pretty easy to pose as a male soldier. There was no photo ID or Social Security number. No one presented a birth certificate or other identification when signing up. Soldiers slept in the same clothes they marched in. Women cut their hair, lowered their voices, and put on the uniform. Many took on male mannerisms like spitting, smoking, chewing tobacco, and drinking whiskey to be more convincing in their roles.

Sara Emma Edmonds was known as Union soldier Franklin Thompson. On the medical crew at Antietam, she came across a soldier lying on the field. The soldier was another woman. "I am dying," she told Sara. "I am not what I seem, but am a female. I have neither father, mother, nor sister. My only brother was killed today... I wish you to bury me with your own hands, that none may know after my death that I am other than my appearance indicates." Sara did as she was asked, burying the woman near the battlefield.

HARPERS FERRY

September 12–15, 1862

WHY HERE?

Harpers Ferry lies in the Blue Ridge Mountains where the Shenandoah and Potomac Rivers meet—an excellent location for providing power for new industries and transportation. In 1761, Robert Harper began operating a small ferry across the Potomac. In 1794, President George Washington ordered an **armory** to be built there, where **muskets** and other firearms were manufactured. The town grew with businesses and people to run them. By 1860, 3,000 people were living and working in the town. Both the Union and the Confederacy fought to control the resources of Harpers Ferry, causing the town to change hands repeatedly during the Civil War.

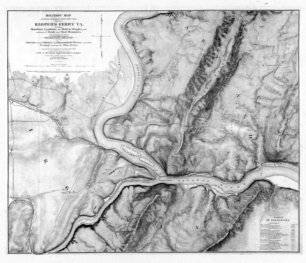

In the Neighborhood

The Union army burned the armory to keep it out of Confederate hands. Both armies dismantled equipment to be used elsewhere and blew up the bridges into town. Many of the townspeople fled the violence and destruction.

The Underground Railroad brought escaping slaves to Harpers Ferry when the Union army controlled the town. They were called **contrabands**, for if they were classified as contraband, or stolen property, they did not have to be returned to their owners. Educator Julia Mann established a school for escaped slaves in Harpers Ferry in 1864.

THE BIG PICTURE

General Robert E. Lee was on the march into Pennsylvania, which was north of Harpers Ferry. He wanted to control the town, now occupied by the Union army, to protect his supply lines. He also wanted to clear a way for retreat if he was unsuccessful. General Stonewall Jackson headed up the maneuvers, taking his soldiers to the hills above Harpers Ferry. By September 15, Jackson had completely surrounded the Union troops below. They surrendered, leaving Lee and his army free to march on to Sharpsburg, where they engaged the Union army at Antietam.

HERO  VILLAIN

John Brown was an abolitionist who fought against slavery most of his life. Religious and fanatic, he made a plan in 1859 to free slaves by giving them arms and leading a revolution. His plan included Harpers Ferry, where he could recruit escaped slaves, get guns and ammunition, and hide out in the mountains. The townspeople and state militia trapped Brown in the armory's fire engine house. Ten of Brown's men were killed, including his two sons. Brown was arrested and later hanged for treason, for inciting slaves to rebel, and for murder. His story sparked another firestorm between abolitionists, who called him a hero, and slave owners, who thought him an insane and dangerous enemy.

What went wrong

Instead of fortifying the hills around Harpers Ferry, the Union commander kept his troops in the lower town. The Confederates easily defeated the small Union defense on the hills and were able to force the Union troops below to surrender.

The Rest of the Story

Harpers Ferry changed hands eight times between 1861 and 1865. All of its industrial and transportation advantages were destroyed by the end of the war. Most of its citizens fled during the conflict. Today there are still only a few hundred residents.

Julia Mann's school continued after the Civil War. In 1867, missionaries obtained empty armory buildings and started the first integrated school, Storer College. Although it was intended to educate former slaves, it was open to men and women of all races. Frederick Douglass was a trustee of the school. Storer College closed in 1954, when legal segregation came to an end.

The Niagara Movement was an African American organization that formed to fight segregation and other unjust laws after the Civil War. The group held its second annual meeting in Harpers Ferry in 1906, in honor of John Brown and his efforts to free the slaves.

Jefferson Rock sits above Harpers Ferry, providing an overlook to the confluence of the rivers. Thomas Jefferson stopped there in 1783 on his way to Philadelphia and the Continental Congress. There was no town there, but the scenery moved Jefferson to say that the view was "perhaps one of the most stupendous scenes in nature."

I was there too!

"The great objects in life were to procure something to eat. . .to keep yourself out of sight by day, and keep your candle light hidden by night; lights of every kind, being regarded as signals to the Rebels, were usually greeted by. . .guns."

—Annie P. Marmion, age 8 at the time, stayed with her family in Harpers Ferry, often hiding in the cellar, protecting runaway slaves and wounded soldiers from both sides.

Lesson Learned

Take the time to think through a situation before deciding which strategy will give you the most advantages.

MUSIC AND THE CIVIL WAR

Just as music is important in our lives today, it has always been part of human history and culture. This was certainly true during the Civil War, when patriotic marches inspired men to fight, quiet songs reminded soldiers of home and loved ones, and the rhythmic voices of slaves sang of hope and freedom.

The Sounds of Slavery—Spirituals

When African people were forced into slavery, they brought rich traditions of music and drumming with them. In Africa, drums were not only used for celebrations and rituals, but also to communicate messages between groups of people. This way of using rhythm to pass along information became an important tool for slaves to talk to each other about their plans for escape. People working in the fields also sang to keep their spirits up through the comfort of music. Although these songs have religious images, the words expressed their personal hopes for the burden of slavery to end. Some songs contained hidden instructions for those planning to escape to freedom.

In 1862, the Union army invaded the Sea Islands of South Carolina, freeing thousands of slaves. It is believed that abolitionists visiting with the former slaves were the first to write down their songs. Since the music was composed by the singers and passed along from person to person, it had never been written and preserved until then.

African American spirituals are considered to be the base of most popular music in America since the Civil War: the blues, jazz, rock 'n' roll, and even today's hip-hop!

Music and the Military

"I don't believe we can have an army without music." —Robert E. Lee

It is odd to think of musical bands marching along with regiments of soldiers, but that is exactly what happened during the Civil War. Bands provided comfort and entertainment when the armies were camped for long periods of time. In some cases, they played exciting marches and patriotic songs while accompanying men into battle. Sometimes, regimental bands served as medical teams, retrieving the dead and wounded from the battlefield.

Armies often camped so close to each other that they could hear each other's bands playing. They would play tunes back and forth in a kind of duel, trying to outplay and outsing each other.

On the night of December 30, 1862, the Confederate and Union armies were camped on opposite sides of Stones River in Tennessee. Their generals were preparing battle plans for the next day while the soldiers tried to rest. Bands on both sides started playing, with songs like "Yankee Doodle" coming from the Union side

and "Dixie" coming from the other. Soon, men from both sides were singing together, when one of the bands began a sad, sweet song.

"Finally, one of them struck up 'Home Sweet Home,'" said Confederate Sam Seay of the 1st Tennessee Infantry. "As if by common consent, all other airs ceased, and the bands of both armies as far as the ear could reach, joined in the refrain."

Despite singing together and longing for home, the armies began the battle at dawn. By the time it was over, about 23,500 soldiers who had sung together a few days before were killed or wounded.

Home Sweet Home
"'Mid pleasures and palaces though I may roam / Be it ever so humble, there's no place like home...'"

Pop Culture and Politics

Music can be a powerful tool—it makes us think and feel. The popular music around the Civil War years reflected the times: songs of protest, victorious marches, songs of love and loss, dances of the day, and longings for home. The lyrics helped shape the people's feelings and encourage them to take action. Here are some songs to consider:

Confederate Song of Love—"The Yellow Rose of Texas"

There's a yellow rose in Texas, That I am going to see.
No other soldier knows her — No soldier, only me.
She cried so when I left her, It like to broke my heart,
And if I ever find her, We never more shall part.

Union Patriotic March— "Battle Cry of Freedom (Rally 'Round the Flag)"

The Union forever, Hurrah! Boys, hurrah!
Down with the traitors, Up with the stars;
While we rally round the flag, boys,
Rally once again, Shouting the battle cry of Freedom!

Confederate Patriotic March—"When Johnny Comes Marching Home Again"

When Johnny comes marching home again,
Hurrah! Hurrah!
We'll give him a hearty welcome then,
Hurrah! Hurrah!
The men will cheer, the boys will shout,
The ladies they will all turn out, And we'll all feel gay
When Johnny comes marching home.

"John Brown's Body" —There were several versions of this song written to honor John Brown, who tried to capture the arsenal at Harpers Ferry in order to free the slaves. The tune was later used for "Battle Hymn of the Republic." There were also southern versions that made fun of the Union.

Old John Brown's body lies moldering in the grave,
While weep the sons of bondage whom
he ventured all to save;
But tho' he lost his life while struggling for the slave,
His soul is marching on.
Glory, glory, hallelujah! Glory, glory, hallelujah!
Glory, glory, hallelujah! His soul goes marching on.

Abolitionist Song— "Battle Hymn of the Republic" (to the tune of "John Brown's Body"). Julia Ward Howe wrote this song after a visit to a Union army camp in 1861.

Mine eyes have seen the glory
of the coming of the Lord;
He is trampling out the vintage where
the grapes of wrath are stored;
He hath loosed the fateful lightning
of His terrible swift sword;
His truth is marching on.
Glory! Glory! Hallelujah! Glory! Glory! Hallelujah!
Glory! Glory! Hallelujah! His truth is marching on.

ANTIETAM

September 17, 1862

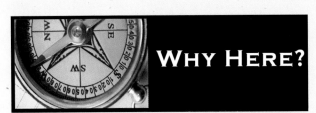

WHY HERE?

Robert E. Lee, general of the Confederate army, moved his troops into Maryland from Virginia in the summer of 1862.

He wanted to invade the northern states for several reasons:

* The US army had suffered defeats that gave Lee the impression that the Union enemy was getting tired and discouraged.
* Fresh food supplies were needed for hungry Confederates.
* A victory in a northern state would convince France and England to officially recognize the Confederate States of America and force the United States to accept the new nation and end the war.

Union General George McClellan was under pressure from Abraham Lincoln to provide a Union victory. This would give the president an opportunity to introduce the Emancipation Proclamation, which would free the Confederate slaves and make it clear that slavery was the true issue of the Civil War.

In the Neighborhood

General Lee chose Sharpsburg, by Antietam Creek, for the battle site. The surrounding hills and valleys provided cover for troops in battle. The Potomac River, separating Maryland from the Confederate state of Virginia, was just three miles to the west in case retreat was necessary. A German religious group called the **Dunkers** had a small white church on the Hagerstown Road that ran alongside the quiet fields and farms. The Dunkers were pacifists, or peace lovers, not believing in wars and violence. Imagine their feelings as it became clear a battle was about to start.

THE BIG PICTURE

At dawn on September 17, the Union began firing one hundred cannons, and the Confederacy fired right back. Union troops shot their muskets into the cornfields where the Confederates were waiting to attack. Fierce fighting also took place near the church and a sunken country road, later known as Bloody Lane. Both sides called for reinforcements as soldiers frantically looked for more guns and ammunition among the dead and wounded.

The battle continued at a bridge over Antietam Creek, where Union troops were trying to bring in reinforcements. When the Union finally got control of the bridge, it took hours to get men and equipment into position. That was enough time for more Confederate soldiers to arrive and ruin the chance for a Union victory. Nightfall ended the battle at Antietam, and the burial crews and medical teams began their work. It was the bloodiest single-day battle of the Civil War, with 23,000 soldiers killed or wounded.

HERO VILLAIN

Many soldiers were fond of George McClellan, and called him "Little Mac." But his popularity dwindled with his poor performance in the battle at Antietam. With Lee's battle plans in hand, he had a golden opportunity to defeat the Confederates but hesitated. Abraham Lincoln was angry that McClellan did not pursue Lee and give the North a decisive victory. He was eventually relieved of duty. General McClellan never admitted that he was wrong. He even ran against Abraham Lincoln for president in 1864 and lost.

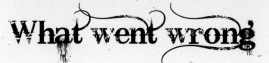

What went wrong

Before the battle even started, Union scouts discovered a copy of General Lee's battle plan wrapped around three cigars. A Confederate officer had accidentally dropped it. Union General McClellan now knew Lee's plans, but he hesitated to act on them. He mistakenly believed that the enemy outnumbered his army forces. After the battle, General Lee retreated with his exhausted army back across the Potomac to Virginia. McClellan chose not to pursue him. His army was equally exhausted. They had both endured the bloodiest single day in the Civil War.

I was there too!

"Bullets flew thicker than bees and shells exploded with a deafening roar. I thought of home and friends, and how I would surely be killed, and how I didn't want to be!"

—Edward Spangler, age 16 at Antietam

The Rest of the Story

The actual battle at Antietam was considered a tie, but Lee's retreat into Virginia ended the South's invasion of the northern states in 1862. It was enough of a victory for Abraham Lincoln to issue the Emancipation Proclamation, and it kept England and France from supporting the Confederacy.

At the end of the battle, 8,550 soldiers were killed or wounded in the cornfield alone. The 1st Texas Infantry lost 82 percent of its men there. It was the highest **casualty** rate for a Confederate regiment in any single battle of the Civil War.

The Dunker church was used as a field hospital. Abraham Lincoln visited Antietam in October 1862, seeing both the Union and Confederate wounded. He offered to shake hands with Confederate soldiers if they wanted to. Most apparently did.

Clara Barton arrived in the middle of the battle in a wagon loaded with medical supplies that had taken her a year to collect. She gave the entire load to the medical staff who were treating the Union wounded. She was on the battlefield during the fighting. At one point, a bullet passed through her sleeve and killed the man she was helping. Clara earned the name "Angel of the Battlefield."

One of the Confederate soldiers lying dead in the cornfield was a woman, dressed as a man. The Union burial crew placed her in a separate grave with a gravestone that read *Unknown Woman CSA*. Her identity has never been discovered.

At least seven women fought for the Union at Antietam, all in men's uniforms.

Lesson Learned

Planning ahead, being willing to change strategies, and acting quickly all contribute to good leadership.

EMANCIPATION PROCLAMATION

Push and Pull

As he looked at slavery and the Civil War, Abraham Lincoln faced difficult issues. He had to satisfy the abolitionists, who wanted to end slavery. But he also had to keep the allegiance of slave owners in the border states, which had stayed in the Union. He wanted the support of England and France, where slavery was illegal. And he had to give northerners a strong reason to support the war.

Lincoln had other things to consider too:

* Thousands of slaves, seeking freedom, had already fled to Union lines. Others were captured as "contrabands" by advancing Union armies. Returning them to the South was unacceptable.
* At the start of the war, many northerners supported Lincoln's efforts to preserve the Union, but that was their only goal. They didn't care for a war to end slavery.
* Abolitionists, however, *wanted* the war to end slavery. Frederick Douglass argued that this was a much more important cause than preserving the Union.
* Although personally against slavery, Lincoln believed that the US Constitution did not give him the power to end it.
* Fighting a war for freedom would give countries like England and France less reason to side with the Confederacy.

Free the Slaves!

Lincoln went partway. He settled on limited emancipation. In July 1862, he shared his plan with his cabinet. Secretary of State William H. Seward wanted to wait for a Union victory before Lincoln introduced the Emancipation Proclamation. Then, after Lee retreated from Antietam, Lincoln had his chance. On September 22, 1862, just five days after the battle, he made his announcement.

THE COMING MAN'S PRESIDENTIAL CAREER, à la BLONDIN.

A Proclamation of Freedom

Lincoln gave the Confederate states until January 1, 1863, to rejoin the Union. After that, all slaves living in any state that had seceded would be considered free.

The result of the proclamation was mixed.

* Abolitionists were disappointed that Lincoln did not end slavery altogether.
* Confederate states were angry that Lincoln wanted to take away their slave property and encourage a slave revolt. They ignored the proclamation.
* Inspired by Lincoln's words, many southern slaves fled to protection behind Union lines.
* The US army began enlisting black soldiers and sailors.
* Abolitionists sought to change the Constitution to outlaw slavery. In 1865, Congress passed the Thirteenth Amendment. It made slavery forever illegal in the United States and its territories.

I was there too!

As word of the Emancipation Proclamation spread through the South, thousands of slaves broke into secret (and not-so-secret) celebration. "The Yankees told us we were all free. The Negroes [visited] each other in the cabins, and became so excited they began to shout and pray. I thought they were all crazy."

—Sarah Louise Augustus, slave, age 8

Art in the Midst of Conflict!

Union Blockades Cause Southern Shortages

Paper, ink, and printing presses are in short supply in the South. To get the news, southern states are working together to form a press association. Information is sent by telegraph from the front lines to the association and passed on to the newspapers. In both the North and the South, one of the most popular journals is *Harper's Weekly*. Although it favors the Union and President Lincoln, its coverage is less slanted than many other publications.

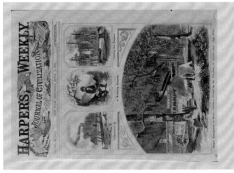

Without computers, television, and radio, the people of the 1860s had to follow current events by reading or talking with each other. They relied on newspapers, magazines, speeches, and conversations to learn about the progress of the war. Just like today, editors and writers put their own spin on events and issues. Illustrations and political cartoons also helped to shape the readers' views. Military leaders were like rock stars of the media. The public followed their losses and victories as if glued to today's YouTube.

Special artists sketch the action from hilltops out of harm's way. Messengers take the drawings to the newspapers where they are carved or etched onto special plates for printing. Sometimes soldiers themselves serve as reporters and artists.

Wanted: Special Correspondents for the Battlefields

Newspapers are sending special correspondents to the front to cover the action and send back the latest bulletins. Those who apply will suffer the same hardships as the soldiers, walking 20 or more miles per day. Reporters stay well behind the battle lines and report the action directly from the field, using the military's telegraph, messenger, or mail service.

Alfred Waud—Artist for Harper's Weekly

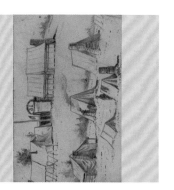

At the beginning of the war, *Harper's* hired Waud to illustrate news stories arriving from the battlefront. Waud is known for his courage; he places himself close to the action for the best view, and his drawings depict the grim realities of battle. Here he is at Gettysburg.

New Medium of Photography Documents the War!

Mathew Brady: War Photographer

The story of Civil War photography really begins with Samuel Morse, who opened the first photography studio in New York City in 1844. He taught Mathew B. Brady how to make **daguerreotype** photographs. Brady discovered that he had a gift for making portraits. He had an artistic eye for setting up the pose, adjusting the background, and controlling the lighting. After he arranged the pose, other employees would actually work the camera and develop the photo.

Opening his own studio in New York, Brady began using **wet plate photography.** Long before the Civil War, he made portraits of important people, including politicians, writers, and performers. He opened a second studio in Washington, DC, to photograph distinguished leaders in government. Many people saw Lincoln's face for the first time in this February 1860 photograph taken by Brady.

Mathew Brady has brought the importance of photography to the task of documenting history. Since the Civil War began, he has sent crews of photographers to follow the soldiers in the field. The teams have cameras, glass plates, chemicals, and wagons that can be used as darkrooms. You will not see actual battle photographs because:

Wet plate photography uses a light-sensitive glass plate, water, and chemicals to create a negative image on the plate. The negative can be used to print positive photographs.

- The camera requires good light, so it can only be used during the brightest hours of the day.
- The shutter speed is slow, from 30 seconds to more than one minute, depending on the light. This requires the subject to be absolutely still. Army commanders insist that photographers stay well behind the battle lines.
- Glass plates are fragile and could be easily broken if wagons collide or are hit in the scramble of battle.

First Ever Battlefield Photos on Display

At Antietam, one of Brady's photographers, Alexander Gardner, took photographs of dead soldiers in the ruined farmland the day after the battle. They are being displayed in Brady's New York studio. People who have seen *The Dead of Antietam* have been stunned by the exhibition.

"Mr. Brady has done something to bring home to us the terrible reality and earnestness of war," wrote a *New York Times* reporter.

A daguerreotype is a photographic image made with a special light-sensitive silver plate and mercury vapors.

Photographs have shown us the harshness and cruelty of slavery, the destruction of cities, and the brutal realities of war. Brady and other photographers knew they could influence people's opinions and feelings by changing the scene in a photo. Sometimes they rearranged bodies, guns, and other equipment to make battlefield photos more dramatic.

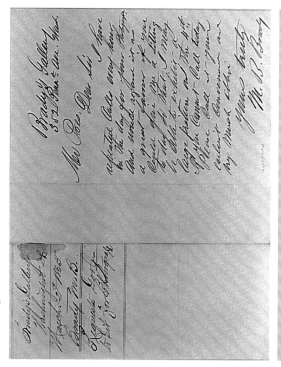

The End of the Story

Brady risked his fortune to pay for his photographers and equipment—and he made sure that, no matter who took the photograph, the credit always read *Photo by Brady.* But he never regained the money he invested in photographing the Civil War. People lost interest in his images when the war was over. They wanted to focus on peace and happier times. In 1875, Congress bought his archive of glass plate negatives for $25,000, but the money was swallowed up by his debts. Mathew B. Brady died in 1896, penniless and forgotten.

GETTYSBURG

July 1-3, 1863

WHY HERE?

In the early summer of 1863, Confederate General Robert E. Lee again set out to invade the North. His goal was Harrisburg, the capital of Pennsylvania. On June 28, Confederate scouts brought word that the Union army was closing in. Lee sent for his other generals to bring their scattered regiments together from surrounding areas to gather near Gettysburg. Meanwhile, one of the rebel divisions got permission to go into the town of Gettysburg to get a much-needed supply of shoes. When they arrived on the morning of July 1, they found a division of Union **cavalry** waiting for them. Both sides sent for reinforcements, and the battle was on.

In the Neighborhood

Gettysburg sat at the center of many roads leading away in all directions like the spokes of a giant wheel. It was home to 2,400 people, many with successful businesses and farms. The townspeople had heard that the armies were converging nearby. As the fighting began and soldiers set up cannons in their streets, some fled to relatives who lived out of town. Most hid in their basements as the fighting began. Some offered food and water to the soldiers. Jennie Wade was one of them. She gave bread and cups of water to the soldiers fighting around her family's house on Cemetery Ridge. On the morning of July 3, while she was baking more bread for the men, a bullet came through the kitchen door. Incredibly, Jennie Wade was the only civilian killed in the battle at Gettysburg.

THE BIG PICTURE

DAY ONE The first day of battle was difficult for the outnumbered Union troops, who had to retreat south to Cemetery Hill. By nightfall, the Confederates had control of the town. By dawn, Union reinforcements had arrived and set up strong positions under the leadership of Major General George Meade.

DAY TWO Lee, confident in his soldiers' courage and determination, refused to listen to his generals' concerns about their position. The battle began in late afternoon, with fierce fighting and terrible casualties on both sides. In places like the hills of Round Top and Little Round Top, the Wheatfield and the Peach Orchard, and in the rocky tangle of boulders called Devil's Den, men fired their muskets, sometimes just yards away from each other. When evening came, each side had lost 10,000 men.

DAY THREE At dawn on the third day, Union troops still held the high ground, but Lee was determined to make a final push against them. After two hours of cannon fire from both sides, orders were given for General George Pickett's troops to march across an open field toward the Union position above. At least 14,000 Confederates took part in Pickett's Charge. Only half survived. The Union position was too strong for the Confederates, and the battle was over.

HERO VILLAIN

Brigadier General George Custer was also at Gettysburg. He was hailed as a hero for leading the 1st Michigan Cavalry against the Confederates during Pickett's Charge. In the following years, he was sent west to fight in the Indian wars. When he didn't wait for reinforcements, his reckless attack on an Indian camp turned into the Battle of the Little Bighorn, where he was killed along with 208 of his men. This event has come to be known as Custer's Last Stand.

What went wrong

Lee was encouraged by his recent victories in Virginia and the Union army's poor performance. He felt the incredible spirit of his soldiers would carry the day. This overconfidence colored his judgment and blinded him to the problems in his military strategy. After the failure of Pickett's Charge, he said, "It's all my fault. It is I who have lost this fight."

I was there too!

"It was about noon. . .The street was full of Union soldiers, running and. . .sweaty and black from gunpowder and dust. They called to us for water. We got great buckets of water and tin dippers, and supplied them as fast as we could from the porch at the side of the house off the main street."

—Albertus McCreary, age 15

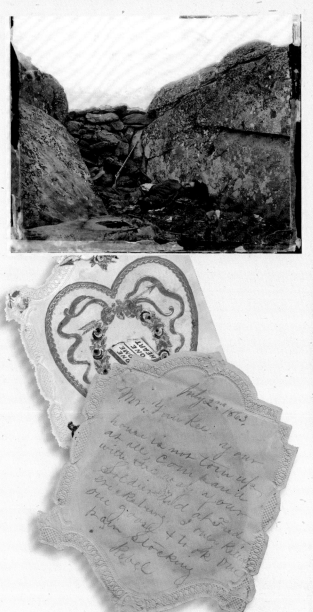

In a house in Gettysburg, a Confederate soldier left this note on the only paper he could find—a valentine.

The Rest of the Story

At the end of the three-day battle, 53,000 men were killed or wounded. Churches, schools, and homes were packed with 21,000 wounded Union and Confederate soldiers. Surgeons set up tent hospitals right in the battle area, some operating out in the open where there was better light.

The wagon train taking wounded Confederate soldiers back home was 14 miles long.

Five thousand horses lay dead on the battleground. Horses that were crippled had to be shot.

The people of Gettysburg suffered greatly during and after the battle. Their farms and businesses were ruined, their barns burned and crops destroyed. They gave all they had left to feed and care for the wounded—Confederate and Union alike.

A Union soldier without identification was found dead on the battlefield holding a picture of his three children. In November 1863, the photograph was published in newspapers and magazines, and his wife recognized it. His name was Amos Humiston. A song was written about the family, and the money from the sale of the music and prints of the photograph helped create an orphanage for children whose fathers had died in the war. Mrs. Humiston ran the orphanage.

Amos Humiston clutches his children's photo.

Lesson Learned

Confidence is a good thing, but being over-confident can keep us from seeing the real facts of a situation.

THE POWER OF WORDS

The Gettysburg Address—November 19, 1863

Abraham Lincoln came to Gettysburg to speak at the dedication of the Soldiers' National Cemetery. It was just over four months since the terrible battle there, and many of those killed had been buried at Cemetery Hill. Edward Everett, a famous speaker, gave a two-hour talk, recounting the events of the battle and the fight for freedom. His speech has been completely forgotten. Lincoln's address took two minutes and has become one of the most famous speeches in American history. Even though the Civil War would continue for another year and a half, the victory at Gettysburg, and Lincoln's powerful words, provided the Union with the will to see it through.

"I should be glad, if I could flatter myself that I came as near to the central idea of the occasion in two hours, as you did in two minutes."

Edward Everett

I was there too!

"The street was crowded with people, leaving only enough room for him to pass on his horse. He would turn from side to side, looking at the people on either side when he passed with a solemn face."

—Annie Skelly, age 7

Another attendee at Lincoln's address remembered the "inexpressible sadness on his face."

—Liberty Ann Hollinger, age 16

What the Words Really Mean

In a democratic nation, *all* citizens have an equal voice. The majority rules, and the people create change by voting for lawmakers and leaders of their choice. Lincoln believed that if individual states left the Union when they didn't agree, then the "United States of America" was a meaningless idea. The nation would fall apart.

That is the message of the Gettysburg Address. The speech honors those who fought to preserve the democratic ideal of one nation governed by the will of all of its people, living together in equality and freedom.

Score is an old-fashioned word meaning "a group of twenty things." When Lincoln said, "Four score and seven years ago," that was a fancy way of saying 87.

ANIMALS GO TO WAR TOO

HORSES AND THE CIVIL WAR

The Civil War would have been impossible to fight without horses. **Think about all that they did:**

* Horses pulled thousands of wagons with equipment, ammunition, food, and medical supplies.
* Horse-drawn wagons carried the injured.
* Horses moved and maneuvered cannons and other artillery pieces into place.
* Soldiers in the cavalry fought on horseback.
* Generals, messengers, and spies depended on horses to get from place to place quickly.

Thousands of mules pulled cannons and heavy equipment. They were not suited to the battlefield, though. Mules were terrified by the explosions and smoke and became uncontrollable. Although frightened, horses were often more manageable in the noise and confusion of the battlefield. Blacksmiths traveled with the army, staying well behind the lines to provide a constant supply of horseshoes, tools, and other metal items needed for repairs.

Feed and Water

Horses and other pack animals had to eat hay and grain every day, whether they were in camp or galloping into battle. Hundreds of wagons loaded with grain were needed to feed the horses and mules traveling with an army. When feed was unavailable, the animals had to survive on much less. Water was another challenge. Armies often followed streams or creeks so that water was available for both soldiers and animals, but on long marches or endless days of battle, horses could become dehydrated and sick.

Many generals had favorite horses. Robert E. Lee rode his horse, Traveler, throughout the war. The horse walked behind the wagon carrying Lee's coffin at his funeral. Stonewall Jackson's horse, Little Sorrel, is buried in front of Jackson's statue at the Virginia Military Institute.

Animal Casualties

It is estimated that more than one million horses died in the Civil War. Many died on the battlefield or as they pulled cannons into the range of fire. Others were shot after being injured. Hundreds of thousands of horses died of exhaustion and starvation from pulling wagons and artillery for long distances without proper rest, food, or water.

"The Horse" by Ronald Duncan

Where in this wide world can man
find nobility without pride,
Friendship without envy,
Or beauty without vanity?
Here, where grace is served with muscle
And strength by gentleness confined
He serves without servility;
he has fought without enmity.
There is nothing so powerful, nothing less violent.
There is nothing so quick, nothing more patient.

PETS AND MASCOTS

Despite rules and restrictions, many soldiers brought family pets with them into the military. Dogs especially offered loyalty, companionship, and memories of home for men who were far away from their families. Courageous and loyal, these animals were often adopted by the regiments as their **mascots**.

❋ The 102nd Pennsylvania Infantry had a dog named Jack who went into battle with the troops. He was wounded and captured by the Confederacy, but he was returned as part of an exchange for a Confederate prisoner of war.

❋ On the battlefield at Gettysburg, the monument to the 11th Pennsylvania Volunteer Infantry includes the bronze statue of a dog, Sallie. She came to the regiment as a puppy and grew up on the march with the troops. Sallie stood guard over the wounded at Gettysburg, but was killed in battle in 1865.

❋ Major belonged to the 10th Maine. He had an unfortunate habit of snapping at bullets as they whizzed by. Eventually, he had the bad luck to catch one and died.

"DOUGLAS"

"OLD DOUGLAS" WAS THE "FAITHFUL, PATIENT" CAMEL OF THE 43RD MS INFANTRY VOLS. CSA. DOUGLAS WAS A DROMEDARY CAMEL, AND WAS GIVEN TO COL. W.H. MOORE BY LT. W.H. HARGROVE OF CO. B. MOORE ASSIGNED DOUGLAS –

Dogs and horses were not the only mascots:

❋ Robert E. Lee had a chicken that accompanied him into war. Stories have it that the hen would lay an egg under his cot each morning.

❋ A company from Wisconsin adopted an eagle for its mascot. Named after Abraham Lincoln, Old Abe would fly over the battlefield, screeching at the enemy. He appeared at parades and helped raise funds for the US Sanitary Commission. He was given to the state of Wisconsin and lived out his life in the state capitol building.

❋ Wisconsin and Minnesota companies both had bears as their mascots. Apparently found as cubs, they were raised by the troops and stayed with them in camp.

❋ The 43rd Mississippi company had a camel. Old Douglas carried supplies for the company but sometimes caused trouble with other animals who weren't used to seeing a camel. Old Douglas was killed at Vicksburg.

HONEY SPRINGS

July 17, 1863

WHY HERE?

At Honey Springs, Oklahoma, American Indians fought on both sides of the conflict, each believing that a victory would mean a better life for Native peoples.

At the beginning of the Civil War, the Union forces left their frontier forts in **Indian Territory** to go east where they were badly needed. The Confederacy immediately moved in and formed alliances with the tribes in the territory. By 1863, the US army was trying to regain its hold in the West.

In the Neighborhood

The Confederates had a camp at Honey Springs with shelter and storage for food, livestock, and ammunition. The Texas Road crossed Elk Creek at the Springs and provided good access for troops from Texas and needed supplies. Union General James Blunt had managed to take over Fort Gibson, just 20 miles away. His forces included the Indian Home Guard and African American troops of the 1st Kansas Colored Volunteers.

THE BIG PICTURE

Union General James Blunt learned that the Confederates were waiting for more men and supplies before they were going to attack his army at Fort Gibson. He decided to take the fight to the enemy. He marched his men all night along flooding riverbanks and over a makeshift bridge toward Honey Springs. At 8 AM he commanded them to rest behind a ridge while he went out to scout before attacking. Although outnumbered, the Union troops performed well. The Confederates, on the other hand, were short on firearms and had rain-dampened gunpowder. Their reinforcements arrived too late to prevent their defeat.

Oklahoma was known then as Indian Territory because of the large number of tribes that had been forced to give up their ancestral lands to move there. Here's how it unfolded:

1800–1820s
Cherokee and other southeastern tribes own plantations and slaves.

1828
Gold is discovered in Georgia. White settlers flood into the area.

1830
Indian Removal Act calls for the forced movement of tribes to land west of the Mississippi.

1835
Cherokee Stand Watie agrees to exchange tribal lands for land in Indian Territory (present-day Oklahoma). Many tribal members refuse to move.

1838
Trail of Tears—16,000 Cherokees are forced to march 800 miles to Oklahoma. Thousands die on the way.

1840s–1850s
Anger and bitterness cause violence in Indian Territory. Many tribe members to flee to Kansas and Missouri.

1860
Some tribal leaders sign on with the Confederates in hopes of keeping their lands.

1862
Members outside of Oklahoma form the Indian Home Guard and join the Union army.

HERO | VILLAIN

Stand Watie was one of the leaders who signed the treaty to give up original Cherokee homelands in exchange for territory in Oklahoma. Bitterly hated by some in his own tribe, he was hailed as a hero by others. He was a slave owner who fought bravely for the Confederacy, although his Cherokee troops often fought against other Cherokees who sided with the Union. He was the last Confederate general to surrender at the end of the Civil War.

The Rest of the Story

Almost 3,600 American Indians fought in the Civil War.

The Honey Springs battle came only two weeks after the Union victory at Gettysburg.

The Engagement at Honey Springs was the only battle in which large numbers of American Indians fought on both sides of the conflict.

Many Cherokees who fought with the Confederacy were stripped of their rights in Indian Territory after the war. The Union loyalty of the Indian Home Guard is the main reason that many were allowed to remain on their lands.

Stand Watie was supposed to join the Texas troops at Honey Springs but, at the last moment, was ordered to another location. He later achieved the rank of brigadier general.

At Honey Springs, Union forces included former slaves from the 1st Kansas Colored Volunteers, who had been freed by the Emancipation Proclamation. Even though they knew they would most likely be killed if taken prisoner, they fought bravely and contributed to the Union victory.

What went wrong

During the battle, the Union's Indian Home Guard moved forward and somehow got between the Texas Confederates and the Union line. They were ordered to pull back out of the line of fire. Confederates heard the call and mistakenly thought the Union was retreating. They moved forward to chase the enemy and unexpectedly came face to face with the Union's Kansas Colored Volunteers. The courage of the African American soldiers helped win the battle for the Union.

I was there too!

"They told us we was going to Honey Springs. Me and my sisters loved honey. We were so excited. When we got there it was just water. We was mighty disappointed! Then we rode in the wagon past the house they was using as a hospital. My sisters couldn't sleep for a week from seeing all the arms and the legs laying on the ground and the soldiers laying in the corn rows waiting to be buried."

—Ned Thompson, a child of slaves, age 4 at the time of the battle

Lesson Learned

Taking firm action even in difficult circumstances is an important skill.

THE CHANGING FLAGS

The Flags of Nations

The national flag of the Confederacy changed three times between March 1861 and March 1865. The first flag had wide red and white stripes and seven stars within a blue square. Because it looked a lot like the US flag, it caused confusion on the battlefield and was changed in May 1863. The second official design had the Confederate battle flag set in a white background. This, too, became confusing in battle, because it looked like a white flag of truce, especially when the wind wasn't blowing. In March 1865, a wide red stripe was added to the design, but the Confederacy surrendered on April 9, 1865. Its battle flag of crossed bars is remembered more as the Confederate flag, even today.

The US flag changed several times during the Civil War too. Even though the basic design stayed the same, the number of stars increased from 33 in 1861 to 36 in 1865, representing new states that joined the Union during that time.

Battle Flags

* Lee's Army of Northern Virginia carried one battle flag only: the red square with a cross of blue, decorated with white stars. Regiments usually put their state names or initials on the flag, along with the embroidered names of battles they had fought in.
* Some armies from the south carried the Bonnie Blue Flag.
* Others created original designs that reflected the state or area they came from. These flags were sometimes used for marching, but not in battle.
* Other flags were important signs in battle. Ambulance wagons and field hospitals were usually distinguished with a green H. Wedge-shaped pennant flags, or guidons, were often used as markers as well.

The Signal Corps

Wigwag signaling involved large flags that were swung into different positions to communicate information. The movement and pose of the flag relayed numbers, which were translated into letters and messages by use of a cipher disk. The disk had a changing code so that the enemy could not memorize the meaning of the signals. The Signal Corps usually set up a station on a hill or other elevated location so that it could be seen from a distance. Battle plans and troop movements were sent by this method, although the signals could best be seen in daylight.

Did you know that when a state is accepted into the Union, the new star is always added to the flag on the following Fourth of July?

CIVIL WAR ACTIVITY

Regimental Flags

Imagine standing on a strange battlefield, cannons roaring all around you and bullets whizzing by. The artillery makes tremendous noise and smoke, making it nearly impossible to see or even hear commands. As you look around, you recognize the colors of your regiment's flag and realize where you need to be. The color sergeant carried the flag, along with five other soldiers whose job was to keep the flag flying. Having a flag captured by the enemy was considered a terrible dishonor.

Project: Create Your Own Company Flag

Here's what you'll need:
- White pillowcase, one per company
- Waterproof markers
- Cardboard
- Pencil
- Scrap paper
- Wooden pole
- Stapler

Step 1: Brainstorm some design ideas. Think about colors, symbols, and images that express something about you. Use the scrap paper and pencil to sketch your flag plans.

Step 2: Once you have your design, choose a name for your regiment that you can write on your flag along with the images you have chosen.

Step 3: Insert a piece of cardboard into the pillowcase so that the markers don't bleed through to the other side. Using the pencil, draw your design on both sides of the pillowcase. Use the markers to color and finish your flag design.

Step 4: Staple the flag to the pole, and display it proudly!

Wigwag

Try creating your own set of wigwag flag symbols, and choose a special message to send.

Group Project:

Divide into teams and have each design a team flag. In addition to sending messages, you can play capture the flag.

Capture the Flag

- Teams agree and set aside home territories for each group. You can use fences, creeks, trees, or other natural landmarks for borders of your territory.
- Each company hides its flag somewhere in its territory. The flag should be at least partly visible.
- Each company decides on those protecting its flag and those trying to get to the enemy's flag.

Rules

Each team sends players across the enemy's border to capture its flag. Company members try to protect the flag by tagging attackers before they can reach the flag.

Those tagged can:
1) be out of the game;
2) join the enemy's team;
3) be a prisoner who gains freedom by being tagged by a teammate.

To win, you must capture the enemy's flag and bring it back to your territory without being tagged!

LEXINGTON, VIRGINIA

VIRGINIA MILITARY INSTITUTE

Established in 1839, the Virginia Military Institute (VMI) was the first state-supported military college in the country. The US Military Academy at West Point, in New York State, and VMI, in Virginia, provided a college education while emphasizing military discipline and organization. Stonewall Jackson taught at VMI beginning in 1851.

❋ VMI Honor Code—All cadets must abide by a strict code of honor: "A cadet does not lie, cheat, steal, or tolerate those who do."

❋ VMI Rats: *rat* is a word used for new cadets. The term has been used since 1854 and is still used today.

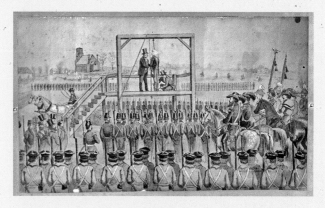

❋ VMI cadets were present at the 1859 hanging of abolitionist John Brown, who had led a deadly attack on the **arsenal** at Harpers Ferry.

❋ VMI cadets were called into service at the battle of New Market, May 15, 1864. Ten cadets were killed and forty-eight were wounded.

❋ Union troops burned VMI in June 1864. Its staff hid important records and survived the attack. VMI has a complete and extensive archive of historical materials.

I enclose you $10 for the use of my son, William H. McDowell, with which I beg that you will have a good Daguerreotype, or photograph of him taken. He is my eldest child, and is far from me. And should any misfortune befall him, I would wish some likeness of him preserved...

—R. R. McDowell, October 3, 1863

Thomas "Stonewall" Jackson

Thomas Jonathan Jackson was born in Virginia in 1824. After graduating from the US Military Academy at West Point and fighting in the Mexican War, he settled in Lexington, Virginia. Jackson taught at the Virginia Military Institute until the Civil War broke out. He got the nickname "Stonewall" by refusing to retreat in the face of enemy attack. Forever known as Stonewall Jackson, he died after a victory in the battle of Chancellorsville, when he was mistaken for the enemy and shot by his own men.

William Hugh McDowell's mother probably didn't know how important this photograph would be in a very short time. While a cadet at VMI, William joined other cadets to assist the Confederacy at New Market. He died on the battlefield on May 15, 1864, just seven months after his mother's request for an image was honored.

Ghost Cadet, a fictional account of his experiences, was written by Elaine Marie Alphin and is based on actual events in William's life.

CIVIL WAR ACTIVITY

Calling Cards and *Cartes de Visite*

Think about visiting friends without a telephone to call ahead. Sometimes they might not be at home or able to have company just then. During the Civil War, it was common for visitors to present a calling card to the person answering the door. The servant would take the card to the person being visited, who would decide if the time was right for a social call. Visits were short, with pleasant conversation. If the person was not at home, the card would be left as a sign that the visitor had dropped by. Many people had a fancy tray just for the purpose of collecting the cards. Etiquette, or good manners, was considered very important. Proper behavior let others know that you knew the rules, were considerate, and treated others with respect.

Some calling cards were very plain, with just the person's name written in a nice style. During the Civil War, **cartes de visite** became popular. These were miniature photographs, taken in a studio and printed on small cards. Fancy designs with flowers or birds also became the style.

Project: Design Your Own Calling Card

Here's what you'll need:
• Blank business cards
• Pencil
• Markers or colored pencils

Step 1: Using one of the blank cards, plan your design in pencil. Include something on your card that is special to you—your home, hobbies, pets, sports, etc. Don't forget to include your name!

Step 2: Using a new blank card, carefully create your design in color.

Step 3: You can make additional cards and try out a few different designs.

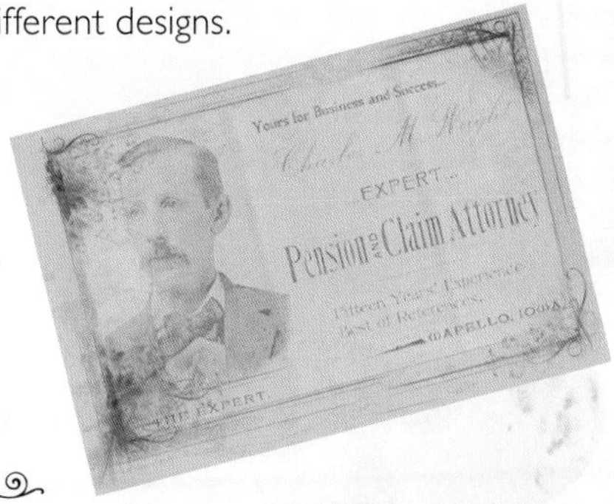

NEW MARKET

May 15, 1864

WHY HERE?

The Shenandoah Valley of Virginia was an important area for the Confederacy. Lee was able to move his troops northward, using the cover of the Blue Ridge Mountains. The rich farmlands provided much-needed food, horses, and other resources. The railroad and canal center at Lynchburg provided transportation. By 1864, General Grant was determined to push Lee and the Confederates out of Virginia.

In the Neighborhood

The Virginia Military Institute (VMI) was only 80 miles from New Market. Major General John Breckinridge knew that the Union army was in the valley. He requested VMI cadets to assist his troops. Two hundred fifty-seven cadets were sent, ages 15 to 21. They were originally intended as reserves only, but the events of the battle forced Breckinridge to order them to the front lines.

The Bushong family had a complex of homes and outbuildings in the middle of the battle site. Jacob and Sarah Bushong, along with five other family members, hid in the basement while the fighting went on in their orchard and wheat field. Remarkably, no one was injured, and none of the buildings had much damage. Their barn was used as a field hospital for both Union and Confederate soldiers.

THE BIG PICTURE

Grant ordered Major General Franz Sigel and his troops to move through the valley and destroy the railroad at Lynchburg. Major General John Breckinridge intercepted Sigel at New Market. Although he had many fewer troops, Breckinridge was able to take advantage of the VMI cadets, putting them into the front line at a crucial moment. They moved forward with the other Confederates, attacking Sigel's soldiers and forcing their withdrawal. Sigel retreated and never reached Lynchburg.

HERO / VILLAIN

John C. Breckinridge had been vice president of the United States, serving under President James Buchanan. Breckinridge, Colorado, was named for him. When the war broke out, Breckinridge joined the Confederacy, and the people of Breckinridge changed the spelling of their town's name to Breckenridge in protest.

The Rest of the Story

"It seems little better than murder to give important commands to such men as [Sigel]," said West Point professor and general Henry Halleck. Although he had military training, Franz Sigel was the director of public schools in St. Louis at the start of the Civil War. Lincoln appointed him and other Germans as military officers to win support from the immigrant population. Making choices for political reasons doesn't always result in success. Grant was angry about Sigel's retreat at New Market and said that Sigel "will do nothing but run; he never did anything else." He convinced Lincoln to replace him. Sigel's military career was over.

The Field of Lost Shoes: Four days of rain had turned the Bushongs' wheat field into deep mud. When the VMI cadets moved forward, many lost their shoes trying to get across.

VMI cadets have marched in every presidential inaugural parade since 1909.

What went wrong

Even though Sigel had the Confederates outnumbered, he seemed unwilling to change tactics when his own were tested. Some critics blame Union troops for stubbornly holding on to their position rather than surging forward, as the Confederates did.

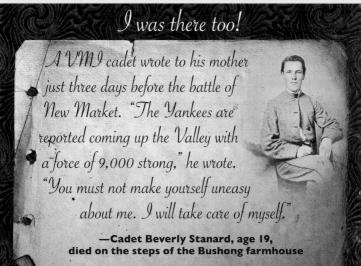

I was there too!

A VMI cadet wrote to his mother just three days before the battle of New Market. "The Yankees are reported coming up the Valley with a force of 9,000 strong," he wrote. "You must not make yourself uneasy about me. I will take care of myself."

—**Cadet Beverly Stanard, age 19, died on the steps of the Bushong farmhouse**

Lesson Learned

Be flexible. Have more than one strategy in mind, and be prepared to change when the first plan does not succeed.

THE FINAL YEAR

By 1864, both the Union and the Confederacy were tired of the war. For the North, the terrible cost in lives caused many to think of compromise and a speedy end. The South was suffering from loss of life and shortages of every kind but still fought on, hoping for independence.

The Union Blockade

From the start of the war, Union ships had blockaded southern ports, keeping cotton from reaching markets in Europe. Despite some southern victories at sea, the **blockade** had a powerful effect on the resources of the South, destroying the cotton trade and discouraging help from European countries. At the same time, General Grant and the Army of the West had captured Vicksburg, taking control of the Mississippi and cutting off another major supply route.

I was there too!

"We have had to stay in the cellar all day, the shells have been falling so thick around the house. Two have fallen in the garden, but none of us were hurt."

—Carrie Berry, age 10, from Atlanta

Total War

Early in 1864, Grant and Lincoln agreed that the limited kind of war they were fighting was not going to bring an end quickly. For the Confederacy to surrender, southern citizens needed to experience the horror and devastation of war. **Total war** meant that personal property was no longer protected; the Union army planned to destroy every resource the South needed to continue the fight.

Grant led his army into Virginia, pursuing Lee and his soldiers without rest in a bloody attempt to wear down the Confederate general and his army. Union General William Tecumseh Sherman was given the task of marching his men deep into the South, bringing the war home to the people who wouldn't give up. By August, Sherman had captured Atlanta. From there, he moved east to the ocean, seizing the port at Savannah and going up the coast to the Carolinas. Throughout the march, his soldiers tore up rail lines, burned homes, and took food and supplies, leaving a path of destruction behind them.

"War is cruelty….We are not only fighting hostile armies, but a hostile people, and must make old and young, rich and poor, feel the hard hand of war."
—William Tecumseh Sherman

Lincoln's Reelection

Lincoln thought he might lose the presidential election of 1864. His own Republican Party was uncertain that the North could win the war. The Democrats nominated former Union General George McClellan and supported a policy of compromise, southern independence, and peace. The capture of Atlanta happened just in time to change the minds of voters who doubted the war's progress. Lincoln was reelected, and the South saw its hopes of peace talks disappear.

The South Begins to Crumble

By the end of 1864, Confederate President Jefferson Davis realized that the Confederacy had little chance of winning the war. Many poor farmers resented fighting to protect the plantation owners' right to own slaves. Some deserted, and others refused to sign up. The citizens and soldiers were starving, their clothes in shreds and their homes destroyed. The terrible shortages and other losses discouraged the Confederacy and destroyed its most powerful weapon: the will to fight.

In the winter of 1864–65, a few attempts were made to compromise for peace. But Davis wanted independence for the Confederacy, and Lincoln would not consider it. Lincoln demanded surrender, a restoration of the Union, and an end to slavery.

THE END OF WAR

SURRENDER OF GEN. LEE!

"The Year of Jubilee has come! Let all the People Rejoice!"

200 GUNS WILL BE FIRED

on the Campus Martius,

AT 3 O'CLOCK TO-DAY, APRIL 10,

To Celebrate the Victories of our Armies.

Every Man, Woman and Child is hereby ordered to be on hand prepared to sing and Rejoice. The crowd are expected to join in singing Patriotic Songs.

ALL PLACES OF BUSINESS MUST BE CLOSED AT 2 O'CLOCK.

Hurrah for Grant and his noble Army.

By Order of the People.

Surrender—April 9, 1865

After Gettysburg, the Confederate troops never regained their spirit and drive. A series of losses, combined with severe shortages of men, food, and resources, created a growing sense of hopelessness. By the summer of 1864, Union troops under General Ulysses S. Grant began to grind down the Confederate army and southern civilians alike. General Robert E. Lee finally agreed to meet with General Grant and to surrender the Army of Northern Virginia. They met at the McLean home in Appomattox Court House, Virginia. Grant was generous in his terms. He ordered food be given to hungry Confederate soldiers and allowed those who owned horses or mules to keep them. No prisoners of war were taken, and all were allowed to return to their homes. Although a few skirmishes and battles flared afterward, the war was over.

Some historians say that the Civil War started and ended at the home of Wilmer McLean. The McLean family lived in Manassas, Virginia. In July 1861, the war's first big battle, Bull Run, took place in Manassas. The McLean home was used for the Confederate generals' headquarters. To be safe, the McLean family moved to a small town, Appomattox Court House, 143 miles away. When Lee and Grant agreed to meet, they decided on this same small town and found a suitable place—the home of Wilmer McLean.

The Assassination of a President— April 14, 1865

Abraham Lincoln was watching a play in a balcony of Ford's Theatre in Washington, DC, less than a week after Lee's surrender. An actor, John Wilkes Booth, was in the theater too. Booth loved the Confederacy. He was enraged by the loss of the war and by Lincoln's pledge to give well-educated African Americans the right to vote. Booth sneaked into the presidential box, shot Lincoln, and jumped down to the stage to make his escape. Lincoln died the next day, and Booth was caught and killed two weeks later. Four others were hanged for helping Booth plan and carry out the assassination. At his bedside when Lincoln died, Secretary of War Edwin M. Stanton reportedly said, "Now he belongs to the ages."

THE BEGINNING OF CHANGE

Reconstruction

The period following the Civil War, when the South was rebuilding and the nation was reconnecting, is called **Reconstruction**. Much of the South had been destroyed. Whole cities were in ruins, plantations burned, and the land scarred by armies. The nation began to struggle with how to best extend political rights to former rebels and to freed slaves alike.

Andrew Johnson of Tennessee, Lincoln's vice president, became the president of the United States. But he lacked the strength and skill of Abraham Lincoln. Also, as a southerner, he did not support political and social equality for southern blacks. At first, the end of the war created a real chance for African Americans to achieve true freedom and opportunity. The Thirteenth Amendment to the Constitution brought legal freedom, and blacks took advantage of their freedom to start farms, churches, schools, newspapers, and political clubs. The US government created the Freedmen's Bureau to help freed slaves find jobs, land, housing, and education. But the bureau was never properly supported by Congress, and it closed in 1872.

In many southern cities, white people were more interested in keeping slavery alive in other ways. Southern states passed laws to take away rights that had been newly given to freed slaves. Many were forced into low-paying jobs, terrible living conditions, and poor schools. Racism and segregation closed the window of opportunity very quickly, not just in the South but in other cities as well. These laws were not changed until the civil rights movement of the 1960s, when people, black and white, protested against these terrible injustices.

The work of living in a democracy never ends. If we want our voices to be heard, we must listen to the voices of others. Although the Civil War is over, the issues of race, individual rights, and equality are still a struggle for some, and they affect us all. At Gettysburg, Abraham Lincoln called the creation of a nation based on the ideals of liberty and equality America's "unfinished work." It still is.

I was there too!

"The country for miles around presented a scene of almost unequalled desolation. Many trees had fallen. . .and those left standing were but a shattered remnant of their former selves."

—Noble Williams, a young boy from Atlanta

Time Line

1820—Missouri Compromise: Congress sets a line across the US, with slavery states to the south and nonslavery states to the north.

1845—*The Narrative of the Life of Frederick Douglass* is published, describing the cruelty of slavery.

1849—California Gold Rush begins, leading to new arguments about slavery in the West.

1850—Federal Fugitive Slave Law is enacted: Slave owners can recover runaway slaves from free states and take them back into slavery.

1851—*Uncle Tom's Cabin*, Harriet Beecher Stowe's novel, is published, portraying the horrors of slavery.

1854—Kansas and Nebraska become territories, sparking more violent arguments about slavery.

1857—Dred Scott Case: The Supreme Court rules that slaves are regarded as property and have no legal rights.

1860—Abraham Lincoln is elected president: Before he is inaugurated, seven southern states withdraw from the Union.

February 18, 1861—Jefferson Davis becomes president of the Confederate States of America.

April 12–13, 1861—Battle of Fort Sumter: Forces overtake Fort Sumter in Charleston Harbor. The Civil War begins.

July 12, 1861—The first major battle of the Civil War: The First Battle of Bull Run

August 10, 1861—Battle of Wilson's Creek

March 26–28, 1862—Battle of Glorieta Pass

April 6–7, 1862—Battle of Shiloh

August 28–30, 1862—Second Battle of Bull Run

September 12–15, 1862—Battle of Harpers Ferry

September 17, 1862—Battle of Antietam: Confederate forces retreat to Virginia.

September 22, 1862—Abraham Lincoln announces Emancipation Proclamation: The document frees all slaves being held in the Confederacy.

May 2, 1863—Thomas "Stonewall" Jackson is mistakenly shot by his own men after the battle of Chancellorsville.

July 1–3, 1863—Battle of Gettysburg

July 17, 1863—Battle of Honey Springs

November 19, 1863—Lincoln dedicates the National Cemetery at Gettysburg and delivers the Gettysburg Address.

May 15, 1864—Battle at New Market

April 9, 1865—Confederate General Lee surrenders to Union General Grant at Appomattox.

April 14, 1865—Abraham Lincoln is assassinated while watching a play at Ford's Theatre in Washington, DC.

1865–1877—Reconstruction

A War with Many Names

Although the usual name referring to the American conflict of 1861–1865 is the Civil War, both sides had different names that reflected the history, politics, and attitudes of the participants.

Union Names	**Confederate Names**
The Civil War	War Between the States
War of the Rebellion	War for Southern Independence
The Great Rebellion	War of Northern Aggression
Freedom War	Mr. Lincoln's War
War to Save the Union	The Lost Cause

How Would You Name a Battle?

Many Civil War battles took place in the countryside, beside streams or in open fields. You may notice that many of these battles have at least two different names. The reason is that Union forces often named battles for the nearest water source, like creeks or rivers, and the Confederates named battles after the nearest town.

Union Names	**Confederate Names**
Bull Run	Manassas
Wilson's Creek	Oak Hills
Pittsburg Landing	Shiloh
Antietam	Sharpsburg
Elk Creek	Honey Springs

GLOSSARY OF CIVIL WAR TERMS

abolitionist: Someone who wants to abolish or end slavery

antebellum: Before the Civil War (example: South Carolina has many fine antebellum homes.)

armory: A factory that makes guns and other equipment for the army

arsenal: A storage place for guns and other equipment for the army

artillery: Cannons or other large guns; also, part of the army that uses them in battle

bayonet: A long metal blade that can be attached to the end of a rifle

blockade: The shutting off of the South by Union ships to keep southern ports from shipping or receiving goods

Isaac & Rosa, Slave Children from New Orleans.
PHOTOGRAPHED BY KIMBALL, 477 BROADWAY, N. Y.
...'d accord'g to act of Congress in the year 1863, by Geo. H.
...KER, in the Clerk's Office of the U.S for the So. Dist. of N.Y.

campaign: A series of military actions that are considered a distinct event of the war

cartes de visite: Miniature photographs printed on small cards and presented during visits

casualty: A soldier who is missing, wounded, or killed

cavalry: Soldiers who travel and fight on horseback

charge: A rush forward, toward the enemy

colors: A flag that represents a group of soldiers

Confederacy: The Confederate States of America; the states that left the United States and formed their own country

Confederate: A member of the Confederacy (also called a rebel)

conscription: A requirement to serve the government, usually the military

contrabands: Escaped slaves who fled to the Union for protection

daguerreotype: A photo image made using a light-sensitive silver plate and mercury vapors

Dunkers: A German religious group whose name came from its practice of baptizing members by submerging, or dunking, them in water

emancipation: Freedom from slavery

federal: A member of the United States (also called a Yankee)

fortification: A wall or barricade built for protection

free soilers: Antislavery groups in Kansas and Missouri

goober: A peanut

green: Untrained and inexperienced

hardtack: Hard, dry crackers made from flour and water

Indian Territory: Land set aside by the United States for use by American Indians; this territory makes up much of the current state of Oklahoma

infantry: Soldiers who travel and fight on foot

juggernaut: An overpowering force that crushes everything in its path

mascot: A person, animal, or object chosen to represent a group and bring them good luck

massacre: A brutal killing of many people

militia: Local troops who are controlled by the state and only called up in an emergency

minié ball: A type of lead bullet used in the Civil War

musket: A smooth-barreled gun carried by Civil War soldiers

muster: To officially enter or be discharged from the army

North: Region that was loyal to the United States

offensive: An active attack

parole: A promise by a prisoner of war or a defeated soldier not to fight again

pickets: Soldiers on guard ahead of a main force; in case of enemy attack, the pickets could warn the rest of the troops

private: The lowest rank in the army

rebel: A person who supported secession from the United States

rebel yell: A high-pitched cry that Confederate soldiers shouted when attacking

Reconstruction: The time after the Civil War when southern governments and

"PROCLAIM LIBERTY THROUGHOUT ALL THE LAND UNTO ALL THE INHABITANTS THEREOF."

economies were rebuilt, or reconstructed, by the North

recruits: New soldiers

regiment: The basic unit of soldiers made up of about 1,000 men; regiments were usually known by a number and the state they were from (such as the 1st Regiment of Colorado Volunteers)

rifle-musket: A musket with fine grooves (rifling) cut into the inside of the barrel, making the bullet fly farther and more accurately

rout: A total defeat, where soldiers run away from the field

secession: The withdrawal of the southern states from the Union

sentry: A soldier standing guard

shebang: A rough hut or shelter built by soldiers for protection

shell: A hollow bomb filled with powder, lit by a fuse, and shot from a cannon

siege: The blocking of supply lines and escape routes of a city or army to force it to surrender

skirmish: A minor fight

slavery: The forced ownership of one person by another

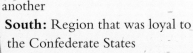

South: Region that was loyal to the Confederate States

standard: A flag or banner carried into battle on a pole

stockade: A line of tall posts joined to form walls, intended to keep the enemy out or lock prisoners in

surrender: To admit defeat and give up

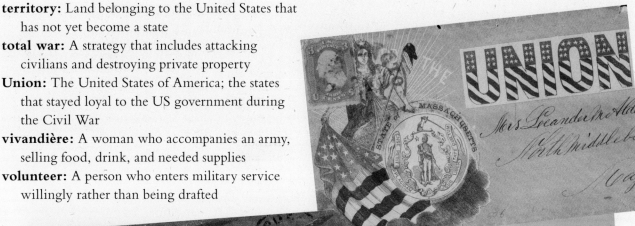

sutler: A civilian who sells provisions to an army post

territory: Land belonging to the United States that has not yet become a state

total war: A strategy that includes attacking civilians and destroying private property

Union: The United States of America; the states that stayed loyal to the US government during the Civil War

vivandière: A woman who accompanies an army, selling food, drink, and needed supplies

volunteer: A person who enters military service willingly rather than being drafted

wet plate photograph: A photographic image made using a light-sensitive glass plate and chemicals

wigwag: Signaling system using large flags swung into different positions to pass on information

wire road: A road that carried the telegraph lines and wires across the countryside

works: Structures designed to shelter or strengthen a position in battle

Yankee: A person who is loyal to the United States

Zouave: A regiment modeled after French African troops, who were known for their bravery and marksmanship and wore colorful uniforms and special hats

Bibliography

Books for Adults

Cottrell, Steve. *Civil War in Texas and New Mexico Territory*, 1997.

Edmonds, S. Emma E. *Nurse and Spy in the Union Army: The Adventures and Experiences of a Woman in Hospitals, Camps, and Battlefields*, originally published 1865, reissued 2000.

Douglass, Frederick. *Narrative of the Life of Frederick Douglass, an American Slave*, originally published 1845, reissued 2003.

Goodwin, Doris Kearns. *Team of Rivals*, 2005.

Horwitz, Tony. *Confederates in the Attic: Dispatches from the Unfinished Civil War*, 1999.

Hughes, Mark. *A Civil War Handbook*, 1999.

McPherson, James. *Battle Cry of Freedom*, 1988.

Stowe, Harriet Beecher. *Uncle Tom's Cabin*, originally published 1851, reissued 2006.

Werner, Emmy E. *Reluctant Witnesses: Children's Voices from the Civil War*, 1998.

Books for Children: Historical Fiction

Alphin, Elaine Marie. *Ghost Cadet*, 1991.

Hopkinson, Deborah and James E. Ransome. *Under the Quilt of Night*, 2005.

Paulsen, Gary. *Soldier's Heart: Being the Story of the Enlistment and Due Service of the Boy Charley Goddard in the First Minnesota Volunteers*, 2000.

Peck, Richard. *The River Between Us*, 2003.

Philbrick, Rodman. *The Mostly True Adventures of Homer P. Figg*, 2009.

Rabin, Staton. *Mr. Lincoln's Boys: Being the Mostly True Adventures of Abraham Lincoln's Trouble-Making Sons, Tad and Willie*, 2008.

The American Girl Collection, *Welcome to Addy's World 1864: Growing Up During America's Civil War*, 1999.

Books for Children: Nonfiction

Allen, Thomas B., and Roger MacBride Allen. *Mr. Lincoln's High-Tech War*, 2009.

Allice, J. P. *The US Civil War: The Battles, Generals, Issues, and Reconstruction*, 2007.

Armstrong, Jennifer. *Photo By Brady: A Picture of the Civil War*, 2005.

Baldwin, Guy. *Oklahoma* (Celebrate the States Series), 2001.

Bolotin, Norman. *Civil War A to Z: A Young Reader's Guide to over 100 People, Places, and Points of Importance*, 2002.

Brackman, Barbara. *Civil War Women: Their Quilts, Their Roles, Activities*, 2000.

Carey Jr., Charles W. *Journey to Freedom: The Emancipation Proclamation*, 2000.

Damon, Duane. *Growing Up in the Civil War: 1861–1865*, 2003.

Friedman, Robin. *The Silent Witness: A True Story of the Civil War*, 2005.

Hakim, Joy. *A History of US—Liberty for All? 1820–1860*, 2007.

Herbert, Janis. *The Civil War for Kids: A History with 21 Activities*, 1999.

Hughes, Chris. *The Battle of Antietam*, 2001.

Jones, Lynda. *Mrs. Lincoln's Dressmaker*, 2009.

King, David C. *Civil War Days: Discover the Past with Exciting Projects, Games, Activities, and Recipes*, 1999.

King, David C. *The Battle of Gettysburg*, 2001.

King, Wilma. *Children of the Emancipation*, 2000.

Marten, James. *Children for the Union: The War Spirit on the Northern Home Front*, 1999.

McComb, Marianne. *The Emancipation Proclamation*, 2006.

McPherson, James M. *Fields of Fury: The American Civil War*, 2002.

Moore, Kay. *If You Lived at the Time of the Civil War*, 1994.

Murphy, Jim. *A Savage Thunder: Antietam and the Bloody Road to Freedom*, 2009.

Murphy, Jim. *The Boys' War*, 1991.

Sateren, Shelley Swanson, Ed. *A Civil War Drummer Boy*, 2000.

Savage, Douglas J. *Civil War Medicine*, 2000.

Savage, Douglas J. *The Soldier's Life in the Civil War*, 2000.

Tanaka, Shelley. *A Day That Changed America: Gettysburg*, 2003.

Varhola, Michael J. *Everyday Life During the Civil War*, 1999.

Wroble, Lisa A. *Kids During the American Civil War*, 1998.

Websites

Association of College and Research Libraries (American Library Association). Primary and secondary resource links. www.ala.org/ala/mgrps/divs/acrl/publications/crlnews/2001/nov/ushistory.cfm

Civil War Preservation Trust. Online lesson plans, maps, student resources, activities. www.civilwar.org

Fort Ward Museum, Alexandria, VA. Animal mascots of the Civil War. oha.alexandriava.gov/fortward/special-sections/mascots

Harper's Weekly. Digitized editions of *Harper's Weekly* from the Civil War era. www.sonofthesouth.net/leefoundation/the-civil-war.htm

HistoryNet.com. Lincoln face morph. www.historynet.com/putting-a-face-on-the-burden-of-war-lincoln-face-morph.htm

Houston Institute for Culture. The Hispanic experience: cultural stories, features. www.houstonculture.org/hispanic/memorial.html

Library of Congress. Digital documents, photos, exhibits, lesson plans, themed materials. www.loc.gov/index.html

Mathew Brady. Biography, photography information, photos. www.mathewbrady.com/portraits.htm

National Archives. Digital documents, photos, exhibits. www.archives.gov/civilwar

National Geographic. Digital documents, photos, lesson plans. www.nationalgeographic.com

National Park Service. Information, battle sites, lesson plans. cwar.nps.gov/civilwar

Oklahoma History Center, Historical Society. Digital documents, photos–Oklahoma. www.okhistorycenter.org

Palace of the Governors, New Mexico History Museum Digitized Collections & Archive. Documents, photos–New Mexico. econtent.unm.edu/cdm4/indexpg.php

Public Broadcasting System. Teacher resources and lesson plans. www.pbs.org/teachers/search/resources/?q=Civil+War&x=36&y=9

PBS—History Detectives. Teacher resources, online videos, activities. www.pbs.org/opb/historydetectives

Poetry & Music of the Civil War. Online lyrics and music (sound). www.civilwarpoetry.org/music/index.html

Smithsonian American History Museum. Digital documents, photos, lesson plans, exhibits. americanhistory.si.edu

Springfield–Greene County Library District, Missouri. Digitized collections—Trans-Mississippi theater, Civil War. www.ozarkscivilwar.org

University of Washington—Digital Collections. Civil War letters. content.lib.washington.edu/cdm4/document.php?CISOROOT=/civilwar&CISOPTR=502&REC=14

Virginia Military Institute Archives. Digital documents and photos. www.vmi.edu/archives.aspx?id=3719

CREDITS

Image Credits

Photographs courtesy of the Library of Congress, Prints and Photographs Division: 2, 3, 4 (far right and bottom), 5, 6 (Stowe, Lincoln), 7 (Lee, Grant), 8, 10 (all but bottom right), 11 (top left, top center), 12, 13, 16 (right), 17, 18, 19 (top and bottom right), 20, 21 (top), 22 (bottom right), 23 (bottom left), 24 (bottom left), 28 (all but bottom right),

29 (top left and right), 30, 31, 32 (right), 33 (top), 37 (left, bottom), 38 (right top and bottom), 39, 40 (top and bottom left, bottom right), 41, 42 (left, left background, top), 43 (top left, center and bottom right), 44 (top left, right), 45, 46, 47 (left, top center), 50 (all but actual flags), 51, 55 (top), 57 (all but newspaper), 58 (right), 60, 61, 62, 63, 64, inside cover.

Maps courtesy of the Library of Congress, Geography and Map Division: 9, 36.

Photographs courtesy of the Collection of The New-York Historical Society: 4 (posters: left [ac03143]; right [ac03059]), 56 (ad16017).

Photographs courtesy of Dover Images: 6 (Scott, Douglas), 7 (Davis, Barton), 9 (bottom left and right), 10 (bottom right), 11 (top right, second from bottom, bottom), 23 (top left), 36 (right), 38 (Barton), 48, 52 (top right), 57 (newspaper), 58 (left, center).

Photographs courtesy of Virginia Military Institute Archives: 52 (bottom three), 54 (VMI artifact grouping at bottom), 55 (bottom).

Illustration by Marjorie C. Leggitt: 15 (right).

Photographs from *The Woman in Battle: A Narrative of the Exploits, Adventures and Travels of Madame Loreta Janeta Velazquez, 1876,* by Loreta Janeta Velazquez: 15 (left), 29 (left).

Photographs courtesy of the National Park Service, Wilson's Creek National Battlefield: 19 (bottom left).

Photographs courtesy of the National Park Service: 19 (top left), 49.

Photographs courtesy of West Point Museum: 21 (bottom), 50 (US Mounted services silk guidon, CWf10ds).

Photographs courtesy of Military and Historical Image bank, www.historical imagebank.com: 22 (top and bottom center, top right), 26, 50 (Confederate flags and 36-star Union flag).

Paintings by Don Troiani, www.historical imagebank.com: 22 (bottom left), 37 (top right), 42 (right background), 43 (top right), 54 (top right), 59.

Photograph courtesy of History Colorado: 24 (bottom right).

Photographs courtesy of Wikimedia Commons Public Domain: 24 (top, middle right), 25 (top), 29 (bottom left), 53.

Photograph courtesy of New Mexico Archives: 25 (bottom).

Photograph from *My Imprisonment and the First Year of Abolition Rule at Washington,* 1863, by Rose Greenhow: 28 (bottom right).

" MAKE WAY FOR LIBERTY !"

Photograph courtesy of Eon Images, www.eonimages.com: 29 (center).

Photograph courtesy of Archives of Michigan: 29 (bottom right).

Photographs courtesy of Digital Library and Archives, Virginia Tech University Libraries: 32 (background), 33.

Photographs courtesy of *Harper's Weekly*: 40 (center, top and center right).

Photographs courtesy of Gettysburg National Military Park: 44 (bottom left).

Photograph courtesy of the Wisconsin Historical Society: 47 (top right) [Wisconsin Historical Society, WHI-1945].

Photograph courtesy of Natalie Maynor/ Wikimedia Commons: 47 (bottom right).

Quotation Credits

All quotations have been taken from one of the sources listed below.

Museum of New Mexico Exhibition Guide—The Civil War in the West: The Confederate Campaign in New Mexico, 1862

Ex-slave Interviews conducted by the WPA Writers' Project in the 1930s, Courtesy of Ralph Jones, Honey Springs Battlefield, Checotah, OK

Stories of Olivia Ray Bruton, www.chris anddavid.com/wilsonscreek/civil.html

Reluctant Witnesses by Emmy E. Werner

Smithsonian National Museum of American History, americanhistory.si.edu

Women at the Front: Their Changing Roles in the Civil War by Jean Blashfield

The Fighting Men of the Civil War by William C. Davis

Daring Women of the Civil War by Carin Ford

West Point Museum

INDEX

A

abolitionists, 5, 17, 39. *See also* Brown, John
activities: calling cards, 53; downtime, 23; housewife, 16; letters from home, 26–27; Morse code, 21; regimental flags, 51; slang, 34–35; spy tactics, 15
African Americans, 58; role of, 8, 31, 48–49
American Indians, role of, 48–49
animals, role of, 46–47
Antietam, battle of, 36–38
Appomattox Court House, 14, 57
art, role of, 40–41

B

Barton, Clara, 7, 38
Bleeding Kansas, 17
Booth, John Wilkes, 57
Brady, Mathew, 41
Breckinridge, John C., 55
Brown, Henry "Box," 8
Brown, John, 31, 33, 52
Bull Run. *See* Manassas

C

Chivington, John, 25
Civil War Gazette, 40–41
Custer, George, 43

D

daguerreotype, 41
Davis, Jefferson, 7, 56
Dix, Dorothea, 28
Douglass, Frederick, 6

E

Edmonds, Sara Emma (pseud. Franklin Thomas), 29
Emancipation Proclamation, 39
end of the war, 56–57

F

1st Kansas Colored Volunteers, 48–49
flags, Union and Confederate, 50
Fort Sumter, 9
Freedmen's Bureau, 58
Fugitive Slave Law, 5

G

games. *See* activities: downtime
Gettysburg Address, The, 45
Gettysburg of the West. *See* Glorieta Pass, battle of
Gettysburg, battle of, 42–44
Glorieta Pass, battle of, 24–25
Grant, Ulysses S., 7, 57
Greenhow, Rose O'Neal, 13–14, 28

H

Harpers Ferry, 30–31
Honey Springs, battle of, 48–49
housewife, 16
Humiston, Amos, 44

I

Indian Home Guard, 48–49

J

Jackson, Claiborne Fox, 18–19
Jackson, Thomas J. "Stonewall," 12, 14, 52
Johnson, Andrew, 58

L

Lee, Robert E., 7, 36, 57
Lexington, Virginia. *See* Virginia Military Institute
Lincoln, Abraham, 5, 6, 39, 56; assassination of, 57
Lyon, Nathaniel 18–19

M

Manassas (Bull Run), battle of, 12–13
Manassas (Bull Run), second battle of, 14
McClellan, George, 36–37
McDowell, Irvin, 12
McLean, Wilmer, 14, 57
medicine, 22
Mexican Americans, role of, 25
Missouri Compromise, 5, 17
Missouri, importance of, 17–18
Morse code, 20, 21
music: slave spirituals, 32; military bands, 32; songs, 33
musicians: drummer boys, 11; military bands, 32

N

New Market, battle of, 54–55

P

photography, 41
Pope, John, 14
prisoners of war, 11

R

Reconstruction, 58

S

Scott, Dred, 6, 17
Sherman, William Tecumseh, 56
Sigel, Franz, 18–19, 55–56
slavery, 4–5, 8, 9, 17, 28, 39, 58
soldiers, 10
spies: tactics of, 15; women as, 15,
Stowe, Harriet Beecher, 6

T

Taylor, Susie King, 8
technology, 20, 22
Thomas, Franklin. *See* Edmonds, Sara Emma
Tubman, Harriet, 8

U

Underground Railroad, 8
US Sanitary Commission, 22

V

Virginia Military Institute, 52; cadets of, 52, 54–55
vivandières. *See* women

W

Watie, Stand, 48–49
Waud, Alfred, 40
wigwag, 50–51
Wilson's Creek, battle of, 18–19
women, role of: as spies, 15, 28; as nurses, 28; as vivandières, 29; as soldiers, 29

Z

Zouaves, 10